T0271650

MAIN CHARACTER

LIZZIE FRAINIER

MAIN CHARACTER

PIATKUS

PIATKUS

First published in Great Britain in 2025 by Piatkus

1 3 5 7 9 10 8 6 4 2

A CIP catalogue record for this book
is available from the British Library.

ISBN 978-034944-209-9

Printed and bound in Great Britain by
Clays Ltd, Elcograf S.p.A.

Papers used by Piatkus are from well-managed forests
and other responsible sources.

FSC
www.fsc.org

MIX
Paper | Supporting
responsible forestry
FSC® C104740

Some names and identifying characteristics have been changed
to protect the privacy of the individuals involved.

Piatkus
An imprint of
Little, Brown Book Group
Carmelite House
50 Victoria Embankment
London EC4Y 0DZ

The authorised representative
in the EEA is
Hachette Ireland
8 Castlecourt Centre
Dublin 15, D15 XTP3, Ireland
(email. info@hbgi.ie)

An Hachette UK Company
www.hachette.co.uk

For my main characters: Mum, Dad, Kate

CONTENTS

INTRODUCTION

Romcoms have long shaped my love life, and I'm sure my age has something to do with it. Yes, the concept has been around for hundreds of years – hi, William Shakespeare – but really, they took off in the nineties and noughties, when I was growing up.

Clueless, Notting Hill, How to Lose a Guy in 10 Days, Hitch, 13 Going on 30, Love Actually, He's Just Not That Into You . . . the list goes on. These films were my guidebook to the adult world of romance, relationships and love. They taught me how to flirt, who to fall for, how to know who's the one. They showed me the telltale signs that someone likes you, how to spot a playboy and the mistakes you can never forgive.

Or, at least, I thought they did. As I entered my twenties, the narrative around the romcom had changed. Instead, we were told, they set false expectations, they were too tied up in stereotypes, they put romantic love on a pedestal. I concede that they do all these things, and I know I've had to work hard to unlearn some of the more toxic messages – and yet, I can't help but continue to love them, in part because there is something endlessly comforting about watching a romcom you have seen dozens of times before: knowing exactly how things will turn out, anticipating the main character's most quotable lines. Not to mention the fact that you can be sure of finding a happy ending.

When I'm feeling anxious, or sad, I often turn to one for a nostalgic hug; processing the ups and downs of dating suddenly becomes easier or somehow more inconsequential. But I also find them wonderful when I'm feeling tipsy and silly, snuggled on the sofa with friends and a glass of wine; or in the beginning stages of falling for someone new, when the butterflies in my stomach mimic those on screen.

I've lost track of how many times I have seen my favourites, but there are snapshots from specific viewings that remain crystal-clear in my mind. Like when I watched *The Princess Bride* with my teenage sweetheart, him holding my hand beneath the blanket, then telling me 'As you wish' in the weeks and years that followed, just like Westley. Or when my mum and I curled up in cosy pyjamas in a hotel in the Cotswolds the week before Christmas to watch *The Holiday* in bed, fawning over dishy Graham. Or when my hungover housemates and I piled on to the sofa in our living room to watch *Sex and the City 2*, critiquing every element of the half-hearted and problematic plot for the umpteenth time.

It was only when I had my own real-life *Holiday* moment, following in the footsteps of Kate Winslet's character Iris to swap homes with a stranger, that I realised there was something positive to take away from these films after all. And even then, I didn't immediately notice the lesson that had been hiding in plain sight.

It started by chance, as many of the best things do. I was in the office on a dark and dreary November day, and it was nearly time to shut down and head off. I opened Instagram and saw a post by the Thursday dating app announcing they'd teamed up with house-swapping site HomeExchange, the one used by the main characters in *The Holiday*, to create a section exclusively for singles in New York and London. *The Holiday* has always been one of my favourite films, and part of it was set at the *Telegraph* offices, where I worked and happened to be sitting at that very moment. I was also single and fed up with one particular man who had strung me along for too long, just like Winslet's Iris. It felt serendipitous.

I'd been a journalist in London for six years at that point, having worked at smaller magazines before making the move to newspapers. I'd nearly always specialised in travel – having used my languages degree to get a foot in the door. Hotel reviews and city guides were my bread and butter. I'd also written about food markets, festivals, restaurants, safaris, islands, beaches, and so much more. But I'd never written anything about my love life.

I showed the post to a couple of colleagues: 'Isn't this such a good idea? I would love to do it.'

One replied, 'Why not?'

I spun round in my chair and asked my editor then and there if I could do the swap for a story. Technically, I would be travelling, so it would definitely count as a travel story, I babbled. The words continued to fall out of my mouth before I had thought them through. She said yes. It was probably the least thought-out pitch of my career.

I'd long flirted with the idea of writing about dating, having been single for most of my life. I had hoped that putting pen to paper might be cathartic in some way. That it might help me process my feelings. Or perhaps the idea had taken root because my diet of romcoms so often included a journalist, one who wrote about their love life. Was I more Andie Anderson or Carrie Bradshaw? Either way, I'd always held back and stuck to what I knew – not sure if I was capable of being so emotionally open, not sure if anyone would relate, not sure if it would lead to embarrassment. Above all, it felt far riskier than travel writing, because it was so much more personal. Any negative comments that I might read below the article wouldn't just be about the story, they would be about me.

That evening in the office, though, I had acted on pure impulse, so there wasn't time to overthink and find a reason to talk myself out of it. And now my editor was expecting a story, and soon. When I told friends and family what I was doing, they didn't find it surprising at all. My uncle, who is always gently teasing me, said: 'That's a long way to go for a shag.'

I found my online counterpart, my Cameron Diaz – Camille – and the flights were booked twenty-four hours later. I was so excited: I was going to New York City in a week with the sole purpose of flirting with handsome strangers. I kept looking at the pictures of Camille's one-bedroom apartment in the West Village – a green velvet sofa, stacks of magazines, lovely candles – and her friendly profile photo, which showed her standing in front of a brownstone in her local neighbourhood, head tipped back in laughter. Each time I flipped through, I'd grin, not quite believing that I'd found someone who had agreed to do this so last-minute, that they seemed like someone I'd want to be friends with, that their apartment was so gorgeous. Like dating apps, there had been other girls I had messaged, but Camille was the one I had set my heart on – and, luckily for me, she had felt the same. The fact her blonde bob reminded me of Cameron Diaz's Amanda felt like a sign.

In other words, my expectations were high. Yes, I was anxious too, worried that I might fly 3,000 miles and not find a single man who wanted to go on a date with me, and that I'd then have to admit that in a national newspaper. But above all, I was excited about my love life in a way that I hadn't been in a long time.

What followed was better than I could have expected: I found a twin soul in my new friend, fell hopelessly for a kind and endlessly fascinating man, and rediscovered the joy of spontaneity and adventure when you're single.

Before I left, I had rung Camille to get a sense of the person with whom I was about to swap places. Her voice felt familiar to me from the off, we'd both been through our fair share of frustrating men who didn't live up to their promises, and her equally funny dating stories made me feel far less alone in a sea of coupled-up friends.

Later on, she was also the first person I told about Evan, whom I met on my second night in New York. At first, I thought someone was pulling a prank on me because he was so perfect. We liked the same films and food, he was passionate about creative side projects like stand-up comedy, and we shared the same sense of humour. He was beautiful, too: tall and toned, with a friendly face. I hadn't had a spark on a date in London in months, so I certainly didn't expect to find fireworks in New York. And yet there he was, and he seemed to like me as much as I liked him. And he wasn't a prank, he was real. It was quite literally a Christmas miracle.

I became just as enamoured with New York City as I was with my Jack Black: it was the fortnight before Christmas and everywhere was filled with festive spirit. I hadn't really travelled on my own before, and I loved getting ready for dates in my West Village apartment while listening to Taylor Swift's 'Welcome to New York' – it felt like she had written the words about putting broken hearts to one side and starting a new chapter just for me. I sang along in high-waisted jeans and red lipstick. I felt so confident, so strong: happy with the uncertainty of what the night ahead would bring. Of course, I also played several Hans Zimmer numbers from *The Holiday* soundtrack, not thinking that when I next turned on Spotify, it would start playing right away . . . in front of Evan. I must have looked like I was going full method acting. I guess I was.

Evan and I had matched just as I walked through the door of Camille's home (having started to swipe at the baggage carousel at JFK – I didn't have much time). I had that feeling of everything falling into place. We met the following evening at a rooftop bar in Manhattan's Meatpacking District.

Instantly, there was a connection: I felt safe with him, like I had known him for years, but the thought that we might touch, we might kiss, we might see each other again had me fizzing with excitement. When he did lean in to press his lips to mine, it sent thunderbolts through my body.

The next few days were a carefree blur of midnight dancing, long walks in the rain and hungover bagels in Washington Park.

There were deep, meaningful conversations, and so much sex we ended up with a Post-it note from a neighbour: 'Please move the bed away from the wall. We can hear you banging day and night.' It became my favourite souvenir from the trip.

Evan loved it too. It was something straight out of a Nancy Meyers film: all we needed to do was elope somewhere remote and romantic, find a home bathed in natural light with soft linens and fresh flowers, and then hang the Post-it note in a frame in our downstairs loo. Our kids, whom we'd have one day, would find the Post-it note embarrassing and fake gag, repeatedly asking us to put it somewhere more private, but we'd still be smug about the levelled-up love we had found. From a dating app, sure, but with a dose of romcom magic. Not that I was getting ahead of myself or anything . . .

In the middle of the night, the second time we met, Evan told me he hadn't liked anyone in a long time, and he hadn't expected our date to be any different. But somehow it was: 'Of course, you live in England. Everything else is perfect.'

It was an incredible feeling to know he felt the same as me, and he wasn't afraid to tell me. His heart was open, never hidden. Part of this might have been because he was American (in general, English men are hopeless at sharing their emotions; based on my fifteen or so years of extensive research, at least), but I think it was also because we both knew there was a ticker counting down on how long we had left together. There was no time for games.

I called several friends during the week, telling them, 'I can't believe it, but I've actually met someone here, and I fancy him so much. Like off-the-scale fancy him. Oh, and it's without a doubt the best sex of my life. But it's also so much more than that. I want to hear what he has to say about everything and anything.'

Camille returned, and we swapped stories of love and lust over chopped salad in a trendy restaurant around the corner from Carrie Bradshaw's apartment. She messaged me after to say:

> It's been so wonderful getting to know you and becoming such good friends these past few weeks! I feel so lucky to have gotten to do this with you. You are, of course, always welcome back in the West Village with me (lol unless Evan's is more appealing).

Her friendship had grown to mean a lot to me since taking a chance on each other online and swapping numbers, and then keys. We had gone on an adventure that never would have been possible had we been coupled up, and we'd found pure giddy delight in the power of the unknown once again.

My relationship with Camille has also far outlasted my relationship with Evan; I guess I should have seen that coming, what with the distance, but the strength of my feelings in those first weeks had made a transatlantic relationship feel possible. More than that, even – it had felt impossible that it might happen any other way. Because that's the thing about falling for someone: it's often so random, a one-in-a-million chance that your paths cross at the exact moment they do. But suddenly, you can't imagine a version of the universe in which they hadn't.

I ended up staying on in a hotel for a week after Camille returned and Evan and I spent Christmas Eve eve together. We ordered in Dr Pepper and pepperoni pie from Joe's Pizza, and then moved on to a bottle of red wine. We talked about our families and where we grew up, our favourite New Year's Eves, and our dreams for the next twelve months. We curled up in bed and had sex on repeat. Thankfully, he didn't think I felt the same as Cameron Diaz's character Amanda, who, when asked what she thought about foreplay, replied, 'I think it's overrated. Significantly overrated.' I will never forgive her for that. I know romcoms don't want to turn into porn, but the kissing-to-bonking pipeline is rarely longer than ten seconds. It's annoying, impractical and, quite frankly, sends completely the wrong message.

In the morning, Evan and I said our goodbyes. My flight back to London was in a few hours.

He said, 'You're not going to cry, are you?'

So I replied, 'No, of course not.'

I pushed the door shut and then collapsed on to the bed to whimper into my pillow. I had been completely uninhibited with Evan from the start, which was different to how I was with men back home. But as our time came to an end and I felt more vulnerable, I reverted to hiding how I truly felt. It was only as we said goodbye that I realised how exposed to heartbreak I had left myself, and I was suddenly afraid to show how deeply I cared. The only way to save myself was to turn down my emotions for him.

I had done this many times before: playing it coy and not asking what a man was looking for or how they felt about me. So often we are told the story that in order to 'get the guy', you have to be a slightly different version of yourself. One that is less emotional, less attached, and certainly doesn't cry – although they might jump up and scream at the TV when their basketball team is losing. The pick-me girl. The cool girl. The 'I'm not like other girls girl'.

Aka Amanda Bynes in *She's the Man*.

Aka Julia Roberts in *My Best Friend's Wedding*.

This was one of the lessons the genre taught me that I can't spin in a positive way, and it's one that has taken a long time to unlearn. I clearly wasn't fully there yet when I said goodbye to Evan; perhaps I never will be. I used to think that by keeping your cards close to your chest and playing the game, you could avoid getting hurt, but now I know you might get hurt either way, so it's better to be who you are. Whole and open and emotional.

Video chats across the pond continued for a while, until they didn't. I was sad for it to end, for him to fade out of my life, but for the first time in a while, I wasn't sad to be single. The experiment had changed something in me and I wanted to hold on to that feeling.

Nearly a year later, I was at a wedding in Norfolk with a group of friends from university when one of them asked me if I was seeing anyone new. It was close to midnight and we were looking up at the stars and eating cheese toasties to soak up the buckets of alcohol that had been consumed. It had been one of those glorious British summer days that catch you off guard: we'd been expecting a chill breeze in the air and a dapple of rain, but instead our skin soaked up the sun and another (and another) glass of champagne became all the more tempting.

'No, I'm not. I'm not even texting anyone, Phil. There was a guy in the summer, but I realised I just didn't like him that much. And since then, nada.'

Phil looked at me for a long second, then said, 'I know why. It's because you're the main character.'

I must emphasise that Phil was just as tipsy as I was. He had that glassy-eyed look that really drunk people get when they attempt to say something deeply profound that's actually a rehash of something they heard on TikTok.

I laughed. 'What do you mean?'

'You were never going to be with the first person you met; that would have been boring. You have this main-character energy, you always have, and so you need to have a few romantic ups and downs. There's a proper plotline, you just don't know how it ends yet.'

'That's ridiculous, Phil. And you've definitely stolen that from social media,' I replied, in between mouthfuls of melted Cheddar. 'But also, I like the sentiment. Thank you.'

I didn't completely agree with Phil. No one's life is boring because they met someone early on, and there is just as much joy to be had in playing a supporting role to the people we love most as they navigate the ups and downs of careers, families and relationships.

But it did get me thinking about framing singlehood and dating in a different way. He was right that if you picture yourself as the main character, your perspective shifts. You can't just be any main character in any film, though: it needs to be one in a romcom. This was what *The Holiday* had given me, that feeling I couldn't name before. It hadn't mattered that there wasn't a lasting relationship at the end of my New York adventure, I had made my own decisions, followed my gut and my heart, and found valuable friendships along the way. I was the main character with everything ahead of them, everything to play for.

I had a similar experience a few months after the wedding, when I went in search of romance on the slopes in France with a single friend. I mean, if you spend your whole life being told you look like Bridget Jones, you may as well fully embrace it, right?

There I met a boy, Max, who held hands with me in the snow and sent me drawings of our imagined future together, and I hoped that we would see each other again. But the trip was also an incredible reminder of how meeting new people, romantically or otherwise, can reignite your fire for life. I came back home and deleted my dating apps, ready to embrace new hobbies and see where they led.

The romcom mindset is precisely the secret to understanding romantic interests may come and go, but that doesn't have to be a bad thing. I mean, almost every film in the genre features at least one dastardly ex. Or a lacklustre boyfriend who becomes the ex. They exist so that the heroine can realise what she's really looking for. In short, sometimes you've got to kiss a lot of frogs in order to find your prince. But that's okay. All those exes are part of your story, but they aren't *the* story. You just need to put your romcom goggles on.

Knowing this unlocks an energy that believes the search for love is far less serious and much more fun than you might have previously imagined. Suddenly, dating isn't a tiresome battlefield, but a big, exciting escapade. You never know who is around the corner, what they'll add to your life, and the places and people and restaurants and hobbies and books they'll introduce you to. You also don't know how long they'll be around for, but you have the confidence to know you can be happy on your own.

Looking back at my last decade or so of singlehood, dates, situationships and relationships, I can see I've been the main character all along. In fact, I have unknowingly starred in my own romcoms countless times, and I'll continue to do so in the future. Some romances even shared similarities with classics of the genre. If you travel back through your own timeline, you might find the same.

I recognise, too, that during the nineties and noughties, it was very rare to see a Hollywood film with a queer romance at its centre, or a leading couple who weren't both white. Not to mention, the action often played out in a middle-class setting, and characters rarely had disabilities. Again and again, the genre failed to represent all people and all love. Some of my closest friends have told me they felt they couldn't match romcoms to their lives in the same way – but thankfully that's starting to change, and future generations will have many more on-screen love stories to relate to, perhaps from films like *Rye Lane*, *Love, Simon* and *Crazy Rich Asians*.

This book is a love letter to my teens and twenties and the decades ahead. To the many romances I've experienced so far, and the ones still to come that I currently know nothing about. To the terrible things the genre taught me that I had to unlearn, and to the beautiful ways it showed me what love could and should be. To new friendships and old, to falling in love, and to falling out of it. To acting like the main character, even when you feel anything but. To helping those closest to you see the main character in themselves. Because sometimes we do need a little help.

In *The Holiday*, it's Iris's new screenwriter friend Arthur who pushes her to finally realise what she's been missing in her love life. And it isn't a romantic interest, certainly not a 'schmuck' like Jasper. Over dinner, he explains: 'Iris, in the movies, we have leading ladies and we have the best friend. You, I can tell, are a leading lady, but you're acting like a best friend.'

She cries: 'You're so right; you're supposed to be the leading lady of your own life, for God's sake.'

Yes, you absolutely are.

1

THE BOY NEXT DOOR

Starring the one who was my neighbour

There is a particular kind of magic in being single at the same time as your closest friends. Especially if you all live together. And especially if it happens to be a scorcher of a summer. There's an alchemy about these three things coinciding that ensures you want to make the most of the late nights and the long days. To bind yourselves together with delulu decisions and side-splitting antics and hilarious stories about what you did to get a crush's attention that you'll recount for years to come. Some people refer to this phenomenon as 'Hot Girl Summer'. Others, and I'm likely to side with this camp, might brand it 'Feral Girl Summer'.

My experience of this distinctive season a few years back was particularly supercharged because it happened just as we were coming out of the pandemic. My single housemates and I were like caged animals being released into the world once again, remembering what it felt like to be wild and relishing every moment of it.

We competed to find the best place for al fresco sex (it's a tie between a grand stone shelter in Regent's Park and a particularly large tree stump on Putney Heath); decided to kiss multiple young farmers in one night in the same grotty small-town club, and then watched them fight it out in the smoking area; broke the law with a policeman (I won't say how, but just know that it was hot); and, of course, egged each other on to send the dangerously flirty text to the inappropriate crush, the colleague, the ex. We really should have known better; we knew each message would likely lead nowhere good, and we didn't care. We loved the drama. We even dropped all our plans one night to go to a specific pub after a friend texted us to say she'd spotted a man my housemate was interested in there. We downed shots of tequila as we tried on each other's clothes and then marched there in heeled sandals, laughing at our genius plan; we sat at a table in his eyeline, pretending it was a complete coincidence we were there, and that we always looked this effortlessly glam.

If this sounds unhinged, let me remind you that in the months previously, we'd done very little else other than binge-watch all forty-one episodes of *Married at First Sight Australia* in an embarrassingly short amount of time, and drink too much red wine before deciding our TikTok dance to 'Blinding Lights' was Instagram-worthy (reader, it was not).

A normal Saturday night back then involved watching the break-up movie *Someone Great* for the hundredth time, while complaining about how horny we were and how helpless our cause felt.

'I just want to have sex. Like, right now,' Shreya would say.

'Me too,' Hannah and I would chime in.

Our twenties were slipping away and there wasn't much we could do about it. The thought was making us restless, reckless and rather horny. We even named our WhatsApp group 'Feral bitches', which I'd like to think was ironic, but was actually pandemic-induced. We knew what we were dealing with was a small problem compared to what so many others were going through, especially as Shreya was working as an ICU doctor. Still, each of us had experienced various degrees of heartbreak during this time, and we didn't have the usual ways to get over it: going out with friends, booking a flight to the other side of the world, getting under someone else. You know the drill.

What we did have were romcoms, and *Someone Great* became the one we returned to most often. It may not be a classic – it was made for Netflix – but to us, it became one, probably because it mirrored our own dynamics at that time: Hannah was drowning from a big break-up just like the lead Jenny, and Shreya and I were the two sidekick gal pals who would lift her out of her funk via the medium of a huge night out with plenty of silly shenanigans just as soon as we could. Importantly, the movie didn't finish with a neatly tied-up love story – it was about the friends who lift you up whether you ask them to or not, who are always there however many relationships come and go.

Hannah and I had lived together for nearly five years by that point, and we'd picked up the pieces for each other too many times to count; Shreya was new-ish to our circle, having moved in just under a year earlier, but she'd instantly slotted in with her wise advice and witty quips. The movie's soundtrack of female powerhouses like Lorde, Robyn and Mitski played on repeat in our house, and when we didn't know what to put on, we'd find ourselves watching *Someone Great* again. It was a reminder, too, of what normal life might be like when restrictions finally lifted.

Of course, lockdown had also made any kind of dating as we once knew it impossible. Your only option during this time if you did match with someone and decide to meet was to walk around a freezing park and have a couple of tinnies on a, ahem, two-metre blanket. And if you needed the loo? Good luck finding one. You'd probably spend your first date weeing in front of each other behind a few trees, which isn't as kinky as it sounds. Trust me. I tried this a couple of times, and frankly neither man is worth writing about.

Not to mention that the pandemic had seriously changed the landscape of commitment. And I'm talking here about simply agreeing to a date and time – the tiniest sliver of commitment. Many of my single friends (me included) were finding that matches would cancel at the last minute, or ask to rearrange just hours before. Suddenly there was a litany of excuses you couldn't argue with, even when you were convinced they were totally made up. But I knew this also spoke to a wider trend; we'd all put up with so much and felt so hemmed in by ever-changing rules and regulations that few people wanted anything serious. I'm talking about all genders, too. The single population wanted the ultimate summer of fun to make up for lost time, and who could blame them?

The most obvious example of our own desperation for this, during the early weeks of the return to normality, was when we turned a chilled Friday night in to something much more exciting on a total whim. Finally, we could leave the house again, and we'd certainly indulged, but we couldn't be meeting new people to flirt shamelessly with every single night. Or could we?

We'd made a pasta dish from the Ottolenghi recipe book *Simple* – a tome so ubiquitous in the London house-share that you could count the number of housemates by how many copies were stacked in the kitchen – and had been drinking Prosecco since five o'clock on the dot.

I have a confession: I've never really been a fan of Prosecco, but there's something about its sweet effervescence that often leads to the perfect level of tipsiness, the kind that shifts the balance just enough to make you want to do something cutesy purely for the sake of the plot. Like leaving your number on the back of the bill for an attractive waiter. Like 'accidentally' falling into someone's lap on the tube. On this occasion, it made me formulate a plan to change the course of our evening.

'Guys, I have an idea. I saw a group of boys moving in next door earlier. I didn't really see them properly, but they looked like they could be cute.'

'Okay. And your plan is . . .?' Hannah asked.

'Let's knock for them, say our Wi-Fi isn't working and ask if we can borrow theirs. If they're cute, we can invite them over for a drink.'

Hannah, Shreya and another single friend of ours, Lily, cackled. They didn't realise I was serious.

'We absolutely cannot do that,' said Hannah. 'They will know we are lying and think we are weird.'

'Maybe,' I said. 'But honestly, what have we got to lose?'

I uncorked a bottle of red wine, and before long they all agreed it was actually a great plan. Or a ridiculous plan. Either way, it was still worth trying.

Shreya and I were nominated for the task. I had suggested it, after all, and Shreya isn't one to wait by the sidelines (a huge part of why I love her). We left the house and about-turned into their front garden; I hovered my hand in front of the door, preparing to knock.

When I think back to this moment, it's like an arty aerial shot, one where the camera pans out and above to include every character in the frame: Shreya and I on the doorstep, Hannah and Lily on the sofa, waiting and wondering, the guys just over the fence in their back garden, drinking beers and unaware of the impending knock. And then the rest of the night happens at a fast-forwarded speed.

First, the door opened to reveal two guys. Why they answered together, I don't know. Perhaps because they weren't expecting anyone and it was already late. I caught a glimmer of surprise and curiosity in their faces, though, when they saw it was two women. They had no context for who we were or why we were there, so I blurted out, 'Hi, we live next door. I'm Lizzie and this is Shreya, and we have a favour to ask.'

As it turned out, they *were* cute. One taller with longish blond locks and an alternative look: the type of man who wears a bucket hat unironically and has a stash of vinyl. His name was Theo. The other, Drew, had short brown hair, a chiselled jaw and a chain à la Connell from *Normal People*. We explained our imaginary dilemma, and they agreed to hand over their Wi-Fi password.

Realising that our window of opportunity was closing, Shreya tried to amp up the flirtation. She made a joke about their Wi-Fi name, Gasmen. It involved implying that they were anaesthetists. While the joke may have been rip-roaringly funny to other people in the medical profession, in this crowd it fell rather flat.

Let's just say our game, which admittedly had never been that good, had fallen off a cliff after months of not meeting anyone new, and despite now being several weeks into normality, we'd not yet recovered.

Still, they said that we should get to know each other over a drink sometime. It was a very casual mention, like when you bump into someone in the street you haven't seen in years and say, 'We must do something soon.' And then neither person does anything about it.

Shreya didn't hesitate, though. 'We're free tonight.'

Her forwardness shocked them. They exchanged a glance with each other, and Theo stumbled over his words. 'Oh, um, tonight? We might be going out. Maybe, or if not another time. But maybe.' It was ambiguous yet promising.

'Okay, well, no worries either way. Thanks for the Wi-Fi password,' I said.

'Of course. Maybe see you later,' Drew added.

We returned to the house, flushed but full of excitement. It felt like the height of spontaneity. We'd taken back control, and the night ahead of us suddenly felt like one where anything could happen. Maybe it'd be the start of a great romance, or maybe it would merely be a strange evening with strangers. Whatever happened, it would be different. And that is what we were all still craving.

The minutes ticked on, and we began to think we had been overconfident.

'I don't think they're coming,' Hannah said.

'Just wait,' Shreya butted in. 'You're being impatient. I have a feeling.' She grinned at me and I grinned back – we are both hopelessly optimistic and romantic. It's part of why we clicked right away. We put on another film.

Then the doorbell rang. A siren call.

We looked at each other, eyes wide, and suddenly we were sixteen again: running wild in anticipation of boys, adding last-minute lipstick, wishing we'd changed out of leggings.

Shreya answered the door, and they filed into the house and out into our fairy-light-lit garden, waving at us with bottles of wine. I was surprised to find no awkwardness at all: the evening was a tipsy, joyous whirlwind of margaritas, music and mayhem. I even smoked a cigarette, which is something I only do when I am really very drunk. I always think I look ferociously sexy when I'm smoking, until I catch sight of my reflection in a window or glass door and realise I'm far from it.

I had forgotten the feeling of meeting new people, of knowing nothing about someone and then colouring in the details. They were all single like us, but they were more than five years younger at the baby age of twenty-two. Next door was their first post-uni home. They had just moved to London and were in the beginning stages of building careers in accounting and events. My housemates and I had all dated men a decade older than us, but our age range on the apps definitely wouldn't have stretched young enough to include either of them. It added to the sense that this would never amount to much more than a fun night – but at the same time, it was also a reminder of the limitations of Hinge, Bumble, Tinder et al., where we begin to impose pointless rules on age, height and more. Attraction and connection can't be calculated in this way.

Hannah staked her claim early on the blond, Theo, practically straddling him. Shreya fell asleep listening to the brunette, Dull Drew. He was too attractive, and that was his downfall: he'd never had to be interesting. Lily didn't agree; she later joined him next door.

At some point in the evening, Hannah disappeared upstairs to tidy her room. She didn't remember doing it, but somehow the carpet of clothes and make-up had been shoved into cupboards and drawers before Theo set foot inside. We later laughed that even in her drunken state, she'd decided it was important to spring-clean before sex.

The following Friday, there was a ring of the doorbell. I answered to find Theo.

'You didn't meet our other housemate, Josh. Do you want to join us for drinks tonight?'

I played it cool and said I'd ask the girls, but I knew we would go. This time we had a few more hours to prepare, so we showered and changed and hypothesised about Josh.

'Did Theo and Drew say the third housemate had a girlfriend?' asked Shreya.

'I can't remember,' I said, 'but I feel like they did? I think that's why he wasn't home, because he was at his girlfriend's.'

'Yeah, they definitely said he did,' Hannah added.

A few hours later, we headed over to their house. It felt oddly familiar to be back on their doorstep once again, though now we knew a little more about what might be in store and felt more relaxed. Shreya didn't wear shoes.

Theo and Josh greeted us with a glass of bold and fruity red, telling us it was from their *Sunday Times* wine subscription. They may have been younger than us, but we thought this at least proved they were wise beyond their years. You must remember that the bar was very low at this point.

Drew had gone to visit a friend, but Theo told us he still couldn't believe the weekend before.

'That was his first ever night living in London,' he said as Hannah slurped her wine, eyes widening. 'He's finally moved here, and now he thinks that's totally normal. That women just miraculously show up at your door and invite you round for drinks. That before you know it, they might even end up in your bed.'

We all laughed. It was ludicrous, or maybe fortuitous. Come to think of it, the evening had an echo of the opening scenes of *The Girl Next Door* to it; okay, Drew wasn't a high-school student, but he was younger than us and in disbelief at his luck.

Soon, Hannah and Theo were drawn together. I sat with Shreya and quizzed Josh. He was sweet, with charming dimples and floppy, sandy hair, and he had gone to the same university as me.

'Where were you last weekend?' I asked.

'I had dinner with my dad. Definitely wish I had been here instead, though,' he replied.

Shreya and I caught each other's eyes; this wasn't the answer we had been expecting.

'So tell us about you. Are you single, in a relationship, something complicated?' Shreya was asking the important questions.

'Very single,' shared Josh. 'Any tips for dating in London?'

Shreya and I told him about a great bar around the corner, and before long we were swapping dating profiles, getting perspective from each other. We told him to change one of his pictures (sunglasses in every shot, really?); he told us our prompts were boring (rude, but true).

Hannah and Theo dipped in and out as we chatted late into the night about music tastes, summer plans – and the size of their TV. It was comically large compared with ours. Did we make a few jokes about them having 'a big one'? Perhaps. Am I embarrassed by this? Yes, of course I am. But not all flirting is dignified.

At some point, I disappeared to the kitchen with Josh to make a gin and tonic, and before I knew it we were upstairs. His room shared a wall with mine, and was an exact mirror image. I considered the possibility that sleeping together could end up awkward.

I had actually already set a precedent in this area. Yes, I had dated a neighbour before, one who lived in this very same house. It had been a few years earlier, when an entirely different group of people lived there. That time, it had started with me asking if he could help me hammer a nail into the wall to hang a picture. It carried on for a couple of months: the hammering.

I decided, what the hell. It wasn't the same room.

Halfway through, I felt that I'd come on my period. I let Josh know, and he went down on me anyway. I was impressed. Remember, the bar at this moment in time was so low it was practically on the ground. If he offered to get me a glass of water before bed? A total saint. If he replied to my text with a full paragraph? An eloquent genius. If he asked multiple questions? An angel, an empathetic soul.

Stupidly, I hadn't brought my keys, and by this point Shreya had returned home and Hannah was fast asleep in Theo's room. I couldn't believe that the tampons I needed were physically about two feet away from me, but I had no way of reaching them. Cue some awkward toilet-paper contraption and a very uncomfortable night's sleep.

In the morning, Hannah and I joined Theo and Josh for scrambled eggs on their deck, each of us wearing one of their baggy T-shirts. When we got home later, we splayed out on the sofas with Shreya to recount all the details. Who had said what? When did we realise Josh was single? When did I disappear upstairs? When did Shreya leave? What was the sex like? Would we invite them over next weekend? Our fourth housemate, Ellie, had missed both evenings on account of being coupled up already, and found the whole thing hilarious. I think she also thought it was rather ill-advised.

That week, working from home, I found that I could hear everything Josh said in his room when both our windows were open, which, given the heatwave, was most of the time. I heard him on the phone to his mum, on important-sounding work calls, and shouting to his housemates as his folk music played in the background. I'm sure he would have heard my *Bridgerton* instrumental soundtrack on repeat, and my long chats to my sister Kate in Australia. He may have even heard me recounting the evening to her, and Kate calling me a cougar when she heard his age. It was unnerving. I decided in my head to not take it any further – maybe I had learned something from before after all. He'd obviously decided the same.

That did not stop me from bumping into him countless times in the weeks that followed: almost always when I was quickly nipping to the shop for a pint of milk, meaning a greasy mop of unwashed hair, no make-up and a hangover. We'd both smile politely, exchange small talk, and then I'd rush off as soon as possible. That's the problem with meet-cutes in romcoms, you never get to see what happens when they don't work out and you have to awkwardly bump into that person again and again. And again.

Hannah was not put off by the neighbour effect, however, and continued her fling as the summer went on.

We also went on night out after night out, my favourite of all being the one when we celebrated Hannah's birthday. She ordered an incredible number of outfits and we helped her choose the sexiest one, taking the perfect photo to taunt any lingering exes and lure in any potential new flames. (It worked. Theo even leaned out of his bedroom window to whistle as she posed for a picture in the garden.)

The four of us (Hannah, Shreya, Ellie and I) went all over London, hopping from restaurant to bar to bar to bar. It was the *Someone Great*-style night out we had been waiting for. We were taking back the city and our love lives. We returned home to find a custom-made cake sitting on the doorstep from Hannah's dad. We blasted music and ate it straight from the box, not bothering to cut slices as we danced around the room, singing along. We took a video and thought we looked indescribably hot licking the buttercream off our fingers; in the morning, we discovered we were wrong.

A couple of weeks later, Hannah and I were sitting snacking in the living room with our bifold doors open when we heard Theo's unmistakable chortle in the neighbouring garden. We quickly realised he was with a girl: a romantic interest.

Now, what we should have done was close the doors, turn up the music and forget all about it. We knew it was not our place to listen in on their private conversation. Of course, we did not do that. Instead, we crept to the edge of the room and into the garden to perch on a stone step so that we could hear better, making hugely expressive faces and soundlessly mouthing to each other. Something along the lines of: 'What the fuuuuuck?' 'WHO is he talking to?' 'This is so weird.' 'This is why you should not sleep with your neighbour.' 'We could both learn from that.' 'Should we go back inside?' 'No, no, no, we need to hear the end.' 'Sorry, you're right.' 'Be quiet, I can't hear!'

It wasn't necessarily a surprise that Theo was dating other people; there had been no signs to show that what he had with Hannah was anything more than a casual hook-up. And Hannah had said to me she wasn't looking for anything serious herself that summer; she was still reeling from her break-up. But she did want to continue what they had for a little while; she liked that he fancied her, and she thought he was fun (and, dare I say, extremely convenient location-wise). So she was intrigued by the prospect of overhearing this conversation; I know I would have been.

It was a once-in-a-lifetime chance to get a sneak peek at how someone you are sleeping with acts with other women. To get added insight into who they are and whether what you have with them is any different.

It started out badly; he told a few of the same jokes with this mystery woman as he had with Hannah. He then turned subdued and pensive as he shared some of his innermost thoughts, feelings that he had never told anyone ever – except for the fact that he'd shared them with Hannah just a few nights before. We gasped at each other; I covered my mouth to stop myself from laughing. Theo was moving up and up on the soft-boi spectrum, and further down and down on the 'people you might want to date' spectrum. It was serious, what he was talking about – family relationships, insecurities, that sort of thing – but I couldn't possibly take it seriously knowing what we knew.

Then the woman said something we didn't expect. She told him that she liked him, and that she hoped that what was between them was growing into something more. A long silence. Then, he apologised: 'Sorry, I don't feel the same way.'

We wanted to squeal, but knew we couldn't. He hadn't said he liked someone else instead, but still, there was something satisfying about the fact that we weren't about to hear him profess his love to another woman. We went back inside.

Hannah and Theo's fling continued for a while, until it didn't. In truth, things ended rather messily. One night when he was at our house, he asked Hannah to stay over next door, but while she went upstairs to collect her things, he leaned in and kissed Shreya.

It wasn't an accidental kiss, if those can ever happen. It was a full 'twist your body and lean over the sofa' kiss. And it happened twice.

It's hard to explain why it happened. There had been a frisky friction between the two from the start, and Hannah had joked that they were better matched. We had even referred to Shreya as the boy version of Theo. There was something too about the way we had all met on the same night, and the fact that we were all single at the same time: there had been so much flirtatious energy in the air.

Shreya didn't tell Hannah that night, but she did the next day. The atmosphere in the house got very weird: words hung unsaid in our shared kitchen and corridors when they were both home. Which was itself suddenly rare – they were avoiding the space that had once been so comforting to us all. For a few days, it was as if an earthquake had split the ground between the two, pulling them apart. I desperately wanted it to be okay, for the three of us to be close again. Maybe there was a way to turn it into a funny story? I could suggest they'd make a great throuple. It would be a

good way to save money on rent in the outrageous London hous-
ing market. Or I could suggest the girls team up to perform some
sort of *John Tucker Must Die*-style experiment. But I knew I had
to let them sort it out themselves. I kept quiet.

Other friends in our circle had strong opinions on who was
wrong or right, and loudly took sides over brunch. Some were
adamant Shreya had broken girl code, and that the kiss should
never have happened. That she should have pushed him away
and gone upstairs to tell Hannah that very moment. Others
were of the opinion that Hannah's attitude towards Theo had
given permission for it. That it was a blurred line, and Shreya
had told her as soon as she'd processed it. What else was she
meant to do?

In the end, it didn't matter what anyone else thought or what
should have happened differently. This was about friendship
and forgiveness, about prioritising each other. And, thank god,
Hannah and Shreya saw that was what was important in less than
a week.

Hannah accepted Shreya's apology with grace and said she
thought the best thing to do was forget about it entirely. To help
with this, they decided together to delete Theo on social media,
and to cease all contact. Their relationship meant more than a
boy who was yet to signify anything to either. Feelings could melt
away, but a friendship like this one needed to be protected. It was
this candid communication with each other that was so crucial to
avoiding a grudge simmering away below the surface; I've tried to
remember this myself.

Within days, the three of us were completely back to normal:
racing to pub gardens arm in arm whenever the sun came out,
piling on to Hannah's bed on lazy Sunday mornings to dissect
each other's weeks, dirty dancing in south London bars like we
owned the place, and lying in bikinis in the garden while sharing
chips and dips.

I'm sure I'm not alone in wishing more romcoms put friendships at the centre of the storyline. Yes, they are always there, but only on the sidelines. A quirky BFF, the queer best friend. Never fully developed – never given the time in the spotlight they deserve.

My friends are some of the greatest loves of my life. They've celebrated my achievements as if they were their own, they've been by my side on countless exploits, and they've pulled me out when I've fallen into a pit of despair. I hope I've done the same for them. Hannah and Shreya are two obvious examples, both to me and to each other. Watching them choose their friendship when they could have lost it was powerful. It reminded me that we must continue to choose our friends, again and again. Friendships need work, just like a relationship, and from time to time, you have to fight for them. Any love interest that threatens that isn't worth it.

And yes, Theo still lives next door.

Some things I've learned about being single

- ❤ Find your urban singleton family – the Jude, Shazzer and Tom to your Bridget Jones – and protect them at all costs.

- ❤ People will ask you why you're single, but never why you're in a relationship.

- ❤ The bed is all yours – and sleeping diagonally feels so good.

- ❤ Make the most of your freedom and time. You may want to dedicate a whole afternoon to making one single, spectacular cupcake like Annie in *Bridesmaids*.

- ❤ You don't have to compromise on pizza toppings.

- ♥ Sunsets are just as magical on your own.

- ♥ You'll meet the most incredible women in the bathroom of the club. The friendship will last precisely the amount of time it takes to wash your hands.

- ♥ Getting with a groomsman is a cliché for good reason: ten out of ten, would recommend.

- ♥ Loneliness and spending time alone are not the same thing.

- ♥ Dating apps are fucking terrible.

- ♥ Travelling solo is a huge privilege.

- ♥ The stories you'll gather when you're single will entertain you for years to come.

2

FORGETTING DYLAN MURPHY

Starring the one who forever gave me false hope

The irony is that the first time I met Dylan, I didn't even notice him. And yet in the years that followed, there would be numerous occasions I would wish I could replicate that feeling, and have him fade away into the background.

I don't remember the exact point my friends and family turned against him, the point where they began to tell me he was a walking red flag. Or when the message grew stronger, that he was using me as a crutch and I should cease all contact. It's hard to remember, because, frankly, I didn't listen.

That's the thing with romantic advice, it's much easier to give than it is to take. In fact, there have been countless times I've talked through situations my friends are going through, only to realise that I've done the exact opposite of what I'm telling them to do in my own life. 'Don't even think about replying to him. I mean it,' is always quickly followed up with, 'But also, I know if you told me the same thing, I probably would still do it, so I'm not judging you.'

One time on a call with my sister, we ended our conversation with a clear plan – she was not to text a specific crush under any circumstances. The next time we spoke, the first thing I asked was if she had. 'OF COURSE I DID,' she bellowed, and we laughed.

How is it possible to know exactly what we should do, and at the same time ignore that voice and plough on? It's because of hope, a belief in happy endings. The romcom plotlines that tell us people can change. And the fact that when you've got strong feelings, it can feel too late and too heartbreaking to shatter the glass of what you thought might one day be picture perfect. And with Dylan, I thought it could be.

He was the Warner to my Elle in *Legally Blonde*; the Daniel Cleaver to my Bridget Jones. I'd never rooted for these twerps in the films, but somehow I ended up repeating this dynamic in my own life. It wasn't that I thought that was all I deserved; I just couldn't see that's who he really was. I was distracted by the excitement, the intrigue, the passion. The idea of who we could become together was bigger than who we were at that moment.

I'd imagined our wedding in a vineyard in France; I'd drawn in the details of what he'd be like as a father. I hadn't done these things on my own; he'd hinted at them himself over the years. Little comments here and there, which for him probably faded into the ether shortly after he'd voiced them. In my experience, Dylan isn't the only man who has done this. Most of my girl-friends have a similar story to share: it seems hetero men are much more comfortable with casual intimacy. They really are happy to say the wildest things – *Shall we have five kids? I want a whole pack with you* – and then forget they ever said them. Or even act surprised that you thought things had progressed into somewhat serious territory.

By contrast, I couldn't seem to let these nuggets of intimacy go. Each time, I'd lock away his words and hold on to them like a magpie hoarding treasure. These moments were by no means consistent, and we never even said the word 'exclusive' out loud, and yet he held power over my heart for longer than I should have allowed. In moments of doubt or frustration, I could remind myself of his words, let myself believe that the reality of who we were and who we would be were entirely different. We loved each other in a complicated, topsy-turvy way. I confused that with being romantic, because so many storylines revolve around drama. I know now that it was not romantic. It was toxic.

It all started with a twist of fate. I wasn't even meant to be at the event abroad where we met, having been asked to go to help host a dinner with less than forty-eight hours' notice. A *Sliding Doors* moment, if you will.

I could attribute the fact I didn't notice him to the jet lag (we had just arrived in Hong Kong); I could claim it was because of the celebrity-adjacent guest at the table (an A-list actor's brother). But for whatever reason, as we sat on that first night learning the art of dim sum, the Kiwi sitting next to me did not register as significant.

The second night, something changed. We were at a grand house for a networking event with a slew of other journalists like me, and PR types like Dylan, all visiting from London.

Dylan appeared at my side early on, and together we ambled round the garden, which was aglow with lanterns. We sampled spicy fishballs (I'll gloss over the fact that I incorrectly explained they were made of actual fish testicles), and did more than our fair share of shots. I knew I should have been schmoozing my way around the room, but I couldn't pull myself away. I didn't want to talk to anyone but him. Apparently, he didn't either. He became my shadow, and one I was pleased to have. When I saw one of my senior colleagues in the loo, I realised I'd completely forgotten I was here for work.

As we left for separate dinners, Dylan and I made a deal to sing karaoke before the trip's end, pinkie promises and all. But over the course of the next few days, we didn't manage more than a wave across a hall or a smile from afar. His grin, which stretched up to the corners of his face, was part of what endeared him to me that week – and it would reel me in again and again in the years that followed.

On the final night, we both knew we had to make something happen or there wouldn't be enough of a reason to exchange numbers. As proceedings came to a close at near midnight, Dylan tapped me on the shoulder. 'There's a group of us going to karaoke. Be outside in five minutes.' And then he was gone.

Immediately, the woman who had been standing next to me said, 'He likes you.' I denied it, not wanting to get my hopes up: 'He's just friendly.' And then swiftly persuaded her to come with me, in case I did end up needing a wingwoman after all.

There were about thirty of us, so we hired three rooms and Dylan and I were split up. I pretended not to be disappointed. Soon, though, he ventured into my room, and again I had to pretend: this time, that I wasn't embarrassed to have been caught belting 'Wannabe' like some sort of strange mating call in the wrong key.

We moved on as a group to a sky-high bar, where Dylan and I took up residence on a sofa, cocktails in hand. We talked about growing up in different countries (New Zealand for him, the US for me), our London neighbourhoods – agreeing to be tour guides for each other – and a series of topics best described as flirtation masked as utter nonsense. Others tried to join us, pulling up a chair and interjecting, but it was like a bubble-gum orb floated around us: their voices were dull and distant, their outlines blurred. We had eyes and ears for no one else.

'Okay you're making me dinner. What's on the menu?' he asked.

'A chicken tahini filo pie. But I'd need a sous chef.'

'Sign me up.'

Slowly but surely, the group peeled away, until it was just us two. It was 3am.

We headed back to the hotel where we were both staying, knowing I had to leave early the next morning for a thirteen-hour flight back to London. Staying out so late had not been my wisest move, but then I have been known to follow my heart in spite of my head.

Riding in the confined space of the elevator together felt electric. It was the first time we were completely alone, and it was impossible to be far apart. If he touched me, I thought I might actually sizzle from the voltaic energy. In a tremendously good way. Dylan was still acting as friendly and flirty as he had been all night, his words often accompanied by impassioned gesticulating and waggish expressions designed to make me laugh. There was nothing I wanted more than to kiss this man – but had I read the signals wrong? That's the beauty of my anxious mind: that despite having had his complete attention for the entire night, I didn't have the confidence to know for sure if it was because he liked me.

'I'll definitely join you for breakfast,' Dylan said, as the lights of the elevator floors lit up one by one, a reverse countdown of sorts. I could feel our time together slipping away.

'I need to be down there at eight. You don't have to do that.'

'I love an early breakfast. So, this is me ...' Dylan slid through the door at a snail's pace.

'Goodnight.'

The doors crunched shut with a loud click, and I felt my chest do the same.

Back in my room, I couldn't sleep, so I decided to look up Dylan on Instagram. I say that casually, when actually I had to unlock my inner investigative journalist in order to do that. I didn't know his last name, but that has never stopped me. We all have that friend who can track down a prospective date's naughty school report and their favourite pasta shape from something as simple as a generic first name. Who can even use those small details to conduct a 360 analysis of their motivations and behavioural traits with all the conviction and accuracy of an FBI agent. Hannah is normally that friend to me, but as she was fast asleep thousands of miles away, I resorted to putting her methods to the test on my own. This was important work: after all, it would hopefully confirm whether or not he was single.

I started with a quick google (read: slightly bonkers, frantic search), typing in his first name and his company. There were a few false starts, including one much older man who initially came up in many of the results. I panicked that I had been catfished, then remembered I had already met this man. Duh. But normally this technique is used pre-meeting someone from an app.

Before long, I found Dylan – in a YouTube video from several years prior. He was only briefly in it. I watched it three times. Now that I had his last name, I had access to his LinkedIn (incognito mode, of course) and a pathway to his Instagram. Again, I had to trawl through vaguely concerning profiles with the same name (a man with his arm around a woman? Panic. Zoom in. Phew, not him. A man posing with a fish? Panic. Zoom in. Phew, not him) until I found the right one. It was a private account, but the small profile picture was definitely Dylan. Cute. Easy. I hit follow.

Unfortunately, this is not the most bizarre thing I've done when it comes to online stalking. I once lowered my Hinge radius to the smallest distance it could go, and pinpointed my location to the address of a guy one of my housemates was dating. Then I set my age range to exactly his (twenty-six), just to see if I could find him to prove whether her gut feeling that he was still on the apps was true. And boom, there he was. And it said 'active today'. I was so excited to have found him, I had forgotten what finding him meant. But my housemate was happy with my work overall. It wasn't the news she wanted, but it prompted the conversation she needed to have.

This category of sleuthing, which is part and parcel of modern dating, is exactly why I categorically do not believe that Rachel Chu in *Crazy Rich Asians* had no idea her boyfriend's family had a multi-million real-estate empire in Singapore. There's no way they went out for a year and she did not google him once. Come on.

Of course, my DM to Dylan showed none of the intense energy of the previous ten minutes. It was far more casual – by which I mean it was painstakingly curated to appear carefree. This was something I had become an expert at in my twenties. I was definitely guilty of obsessing over the construction of each message in the beginning stages of getting to know someone. Of carefully choosing each word, asking a friend's opinion on tone. Even if it was just one sentence. Because every word meant something and could change the course of their reply, and thus your life. At least, that's what I thought. Now I know that learning to let yourself say exactly what you want, to be exactly who you are, is so fucking liberating.

I typed:

> Realised there are like four different breakfast places – so if you do make it down for 8 and I'll be impressed if you do haha – let me know which one.

The message was perfect, because if he didn't reply, I hadn't revealed too much of myself, so it wouldn't be embarrassing. It also meant he had a get-out card that wouldn't hurt my feelings, as he could just say he didn't see it until the morning.

I need not have worried, as his reply was near instant:

> Let's try them all! I'm totally not ready for sleep yet, and breakfast starts at 6ish. How about hanging out/just heading to breakfast now?

Before I knew it, he was in my room, under the guise of using the minibar until the buffet opened. We popped a bottle of something fizzy, and stepped on to the balcony. The lights of Hong Kong twinkled. I was happy.

Later we retreated inside and collapsed on the bed, fully

clothed, and took turns choosing music. He introduced me to his favourite Kiwi musicians, including Mako Road; I played him Spanish and French pop like Aya Nakamura. Our faces were inches away – but still no kiss.

We never made it to the breakfast buffet that morning, choosing instead to lie next to each other, softly chatting and napping until I had to stuff my belongings into my bag and leave. There was no kiss; no fireworks moment. A polite hug, a 'nice to meet you'. Had I imagined it all?

On the way to the airport, I didn't have time to overthink it, as instead I was trying to figure out if I was still drunk or already hungover – the serious lack of sleep was not helping. The plane journey was no better. It was my first time in first class – and I spent most of it in the toilet. Throwing up.

Of course, as soon as Dylan was back in London, I knew that I hadn't imagined the connection. But what I could never understand was that even though he had been so kind while we were away, acting like the perfect gentleman and not making a move when he so easily could have, that behaviour didn't quite translate to London.

And so began months (and then years) of mixed messages. He was near impossible to nail down on a time and a place, and even then, there was a fifty-fifty chance it would end in complete disappointment. On our very first date, we met in a pub in my neighbourhood. After half an hour, he said he had to leave to finish work before the morning. I thought he was joking; we had texted for weeks to agree a date. Again there was no kiss, no fireworks moment. I watched him whizz away in an Uber and felt like a complete fool.

I returned home and prayed my housemates would be in to pull me out of my funk. They were, and as soon as they heard my key in the door they sprang into action, sensing that something had gone wrong if I was back so soon. They consoled me with hopeful excuses that they didn't fully believe to explain his behaviour. Even when you can tell that your friends are bending the truth to make you feel better, it still feels so comforting.

'Just wait and see,' Hannah said. 'Maybe he really did have work?'

'Maybe he realised he didn't like me in person as much as he thought he did,' I said.

'Shut up,' Hannah replied.

They all gave me advice on next steps.

'Whatever you do, don't message him first.'

'Let's go out tomorrow, and we'll get a hot pic of you to post.'

'Yeah and we could even angle it to get a man's chunky legs in the background to make it seem like you're on a date.'

'That will have him crawling back in no time.'

But I didn't end up needing it, because within an hour, he'd messaged me to ask whether I wanted to go to his when he was done with emails. I thought it was strange. Was that the only reason he had turned up earlier? To make this seem like less of a booty call? I didn't go. It didn't feel right. That could have been the end, only he didn't take it personally that I stayed at home. We continued to message, and soon we'd planned another time to meet up. Finally, the first kiss happened, and it was quickly followed by a second and a third. We were hungry for each other, and it had been worth the wait. Though in the weeks that followed I still wasn't sure where we stood thanks to more of the behaviour I'd experienced on that first date.

His favourite trick was to suggest doing something on any given day, and then, as it got closer to the time we were due to meet, he'd say work meant he needed to push it back by thirty minutes, then an hour, and it would just go on and on. Sometimes he was so late, he'd order an Uber to my house to take me straight to his, skipping out the bar or restaurant altogether.

Sometimes I still went, sometimes I didn't. I certainly never brought a toothbrush.

This banal everyday object has become the ultimate symbol for

'Hey, wink wink, I know I'm spending the night,' and for some reason, even when it's obvious to all parties involved that this is absolutely what you will be doing, it can feel like a gigantic step too far. I've got over that since. Now I might even bring a silk eye mask in my handbag. Sleep is far more important to me than ridiculous pretences. This is what rebelling looks like in your thirties.

I blame our first week together in Asia for why I put up with all the ups and downs. He hadn't jumped at sleeping with me then, or even kissed me, so I felt like it couldn't be that he wanted to see me just for sex. And, of course, there were good times too. He always knew the precise moment when I was finally ready to call it quits, and suddenly he would pop up and be all charming and stupid cute again. It was like a bat signal. He's not the only one; too many men seem to have this instinct. It's as if an alarm goes off in their brain at the exact moment you're about to slip away: 'Alert, alert. You're about to lose her. Spring into action.' In his case, he would choose these moments to reappear as that spontaneous, fun, but most of all kind man that I had fallen for in a hotel in Hong Kong. And I'd forget why I ever wanted to end it.

A steak dinner and a beautiful bottle of red he'd insisted on splashing out on in a local French restaurant, where my cheeks felt rosy the entire night from all the wine and smiling. The Saturday morning when I left after staying at his, only to receive a text a couple of hours later asking me to return. We spent the rest of the weekend cooking, watching terribly corny low-budget Christmas romcoms, chatting silliness and lying intertwined like a naked puzzle. The evening at the cinema, where I handed him my knickers as we took our seats, and the astonishing sex that followed hours of anticipation. The time I cried to him on the phone as the pandemic took hold, and how he knew exactly what to say despite his own world being turned upside down.

These were the moments I chose to remember, that I held on to for too long. When I look back on it now, years later, and force myself to think of the reality, I know that our entire relationship was always on his terms.

Perhaps 'relationship' is too grand a word. I should have really labelled it as a situationship: what we had was intimacy without commitment, rapport without stability, in-jokes and pet names without growth.

I'd like to say the pandemic was the final nail in the coffin for us, that it ruined what we had by separating us for months. The truth is, it allowed us to prolong the inevitable with long phone calls and messages – and meant there was a reason I couldn't argue with for why we couldn't meet.

When the first lockdown finally lifted and I returned to London, having stayed with my mum in the countryside for the duration, I couldn't wait to hold his hand, to kiss his face, to see his smile. He'd said the same to me. While it had been months since we had last seen each other, I felt just as close to him. We'd had deep conversations that went on late into the night, we'd flirted endlessly, and we'd had more than a few sexy video calls. One time it was a hot summer's day and I'd been sunbathing, but I nipped inside to strip off my swimsuit. The moment could have been ruined by the fact my mum pushed open the door to my room to say she'd made me a ham sandwich just as he started to come, but instead we found it hilarious. I'm still not sure if she knew entirely what was going on, other than the fact I was naked and didn't want her in there. I guess she will do now. Whoops.

And yet, as I returned to London, he became distant again, vague once more about dates and timings.

He was not in a good place: his father was ill and in a country far away. I tried to speak to him on the phone, but he wouldn't answer, so I sent a message telling him I was sorry for what was happening and that I wanted to be the person to support him, but it also felt like this was something he wanted to handle on his own, so I needed to step away. Hannah helped me compose the message – we must have come up with ten different iterations before settling on the perfect choice of words. I can picture her perched on my bed, me at my desk, the anxiety bubbling away within me.

'No, don't send it yet. You need a full stop there,' she said.

'It doesn't really matter.' I was on the brink of tears – the ones that stream out of the corners of your eyes without a sound. There was no sobbing soundtrack, just quiet desperation.

'It does. He needs to know this is the end and that he hasn't been fair to you.'

'Okay,' I said meekly.

He never replied. I was shocked. This was someone I had known for nearly a year now; I had shared so much with him, and him with me. At that time, I never thought there was a chance he wouldn't say anything. I wasn't expecting a big romantic gesture, for him to sit with a boombox outside my window and tell me he didn't want to ruin his chances. I didn't expect him to send me a pizza with 'Sorry' spelled out in M&M's. I didn't even really want him to do any of those things; grand gestures as an apology have always felt like too little too late to me. Even when they really are very grand. Anyone can do something like that once if they really try, but it doesn't matter or mean anything if they don't then provide the reassurance and love you need on a day-to-day basis.

That's not to say I don't like someone planning a surprise, nor that I wouldn't enjoy orchestrating one myself. But these gestures are best when they are fun and spontaneous, when they happen on the most normal of days, when there is no reason for them. No guilty face behind them. But, of course, in this case it didn't matter what I thought, because there would be no grand gesture. There would be no small gesture, either. I thought Dylan would at least say sorry and maybe send a generic 'wish you all the best' message. I was wrong.

It was *Sliding Doors* all over again. I cycled through the not-quite relationship in my head for weeks afterwards, wondering what tiny details would need to have changed in order for the result to be different. If the pandemic hadn't happened. If his dad hadn't been ill. If he hadn't missed that promotion. If I hadn't gone to the countryside. If I had been passed over at *my* work. If I'd said yes that time he asked me to go round to his. Maybe it would all have been different. I wasn't ready yet to accept that the result would always have been the same.

At first I was sad. Really, really sad. Disillusioned. Distraught. Deceived. And then I was angry, mainly that he hadn't even replied. I had laid bare my whole heart. He thought that an appropriate reaction was silence.

I called my dad, and he knew as soon as he picked up that something was wrong. My heavy breathing on the other end of the line and inability to get my words out was the first sign. We speak often on the phone because we live in different countries, and he always knows exactly what to say when I am heartbroken. Whether to be sincere or to crack a joke about how shit men are. He'll start with: 'Take a breath. Will it matter in five years? Think about it and you'll feel calmer.' Then he'll quickly segue into his other go-to line: 'At the end of the day, when it comes to sex, all men are pigs.' No matter how many times I've heard him say these exact phrases, it instantly makes me feel better.

My dad will also remind me that there are pluses and minuses to being in a relationship. That he too has had his fair share of heartbreak, but he's got through it. He will then always remind me of divorce rates in several different countries, including the US and the UK.

'That's not exactly what I want to hear,' I say.

'I know, but I'm reminding you that just because someone is married, it doesn't mean they are happier.'

It wasn't until several months later that Dylan finally got in touch. I'd seen on Instagram that he'd moved back to New Zealand to spend time with his dad, but that was the extent of what I knew.

I was walking in Soho and felt my phone buzz, so I pulled it out to look, but never expected it to be him. Seeing his name light up the screen stopped me in my tracks and sent shockwaves through my body. He'd started by replying to a story I'd posted; the night before, I'd stayed in a new hotel for work (coincidentally, an off-shoot of the same brand we'd stayed at in Hong Kong). It was a trivial message to test the waters and see if I would reply:

> Is that a teapot/alarm clock?!

I responded:

> Why are you messaging me, you pathetic bastard? I have no more time for you and your Peter Pan antics.

Just kidding. Of course I didn't say that.

Instead, I said something droll about the snazzy toilet (we had both loved the high-tech loos with waterfall sound effects on our trip), as if we had never stopped talking.

Then he hit me with the following:

> Doing a lot of reflection and thinking about you a bit. Sure you know that you're amazing and should be told every day.

There were questions too about how I was and what I was doing for Christmas.

I stared at the locked screen in disbelief and shook my head. It made me enormously happy, and the warming glow of nostalgia swept over me, but I also felt a deep sadness that he hadn't come to this realisation before. I needed to speak to The Council (aka my closest friends) before opening the message or replying further.

I called several of them in quick succession: Hannah, Jess,

Nick, Alice, my sister and more. Different friends, different conversations, slightly different takes – but they were all unanimous in warning me, 'Do not reply.' I swore to them that if I did reply – which I might, because that would be polite and I obviously wanted to know what had triggered this delayed response – I wouldn't fall for him again. All the while, I was aware there was a strong chance I would.

And I did manage to not reply . . . for a day. I knew that ultimately I would, but I wanted to think it through properly first, to decide how open I wanted to leave the door. But before I could, he shot through another:

> Guess not. Still stand by the statement that you're amazing. Keep being yourself xxx.

Any nostalgia I had felt turned to anger. He was trying to be playful, sure, but how dare he be rude to me for not replying within twenty-four hours when he had done the same to me for months?

I wrote:

> I was out last night so didn't have a chance to reply. Also quite unfair, Dylan, given you never acknowledged my last message to you in July. It feels a bit late and out of the blue. You never really made me feel like you thought I was amazing.

I seethed and I seethed. I vowed to never talk to him again. And then, against my better judgement, on Christmas Day, I sent him a message saying:

> Happy Christmas Dylan xx

What is it about the holidays that makes us reflect, that causes us to want to make amends? I had too much time to think thanks to the days off, and I found myself wondering if I had been too harsh. I didn't approach The Council before sending my Christmas text; I knew they would not approve. I had chatted through the details with my mum, though, as we marched through mud on a long countryside walk. She wasn't a fan of Dylan, knowing how often he picked me up and then dropped me again, but she also knew how much he had meant to me.

He replied, wishing me a happy Christmas too, and letting me know his dad had passed away. I burst into tears. I knew what a close relationship they'd had and that he had done everything he could to be there for him in the last months of his life, sitting and holding his hand, telling him stories. I may not have known his dad, but I still cared for Dylan deeply and wished there was something I could do or say that would be a comfort.

I couldn't hold on to the anger towards him any longer: the feelings that had been there since we'd first met bubbled back up. I accepted his apologies.

Every few months, for the next two years – and yes, it pains me to write that it went on that long – he'd suddenly be in my DMs again. Often with emojis. A flame. Heart eyes. My housemates started to call him 'emoji man'. I hated that my heart still skipped a beat when his name flashed up on my phone.

Then the texts would come, followed by the phone calls. The latter were always when he was at his most emotional, his most vulnerable. During one particularly long one, he told me whenever he thought about his future, who his life partner would be, I had every characteristic he was looking for. I cried silently: these were the words I'd wanted to hear for so long.

I'm not innocent in this, either. When I went on a boring date and felt exasperated – because I couldn't feel a spark, and I had spiralled that maybe I wouldn't ever connect with someone again like I had with Dylan – I'd message him, knowing the serotonin boost it would give me. It was true we were both using each other, but the difference was that I would have jumped on a plane to see him in an instant. His words were just that: words.

The last call like this I received from Dylan was in the summer before I visited Australia, where my sister lives. He told me he wasn't in the happiest place, that he felt like an outsider in New Zealand. 'I don't know, I just feel that I haven't made any real connections here. It's where I'm from but I don't know that I belong here anymore.' He paused before continuing, 'I've been thinking about maybe moving back to Europe.'

I didn't know what to say, as obviously I wanted him back in London with me, but ultimately that was his decision to make, not mine. I also couldn't help but feel that what he was really looking for was an ego boost. He needed me to make him feel wanted. He might have known deep down that he wouldn't move back, but he could play with the idea of it – and play with the idea of me, too. And he would feel good knowing I was still an option, that I still thought he was attractive. It was selfish and absurd. I asked him, 'Why did you call me to tell me this?'

He said I was the only person who knew how to make him feel better when he was low.

By this point, I had more of a backbone: 'Dylan, you can't just keep saying these big emotional things to me without action. The borders are open now, but I don't see you booking a flight.' I had grown numb to his emotional manipulation; his words didn't mean anything. Or at least I could pretend this was the case – which was progress, in my own way.

'Hey, hey, look, I am planning on coming to Europe soon. I just need to sort a few things out. You'll be the first person to know, trust me,' he said.

I can't remember what his specific excuses were, what it was that he needed to sort out. I can't remember the excuses, because I'm sure they weren't true.

A few days later, I messaged him to tell him I had booked flights to see my sister. He'd known the trip was on the cards, but now I had an actual date. Soon, I would be on the same side of the world as him again, after years apart. We would even be visiting New Zealand while I was there. This was his chance to show me he had changed. But, what a surprise, the weeks that followed were filled once again with radio silence. I went for drinks on a rooftop with Hannah and, with her encouragement, I wrote:

> The fact you haven't replied to this reiterates what I said during our phone call last week.

And yet, I still couldn't get him out of my head. The thought of being in the very same city as him after so long and not meeting felt wild. So, despite everyone's advice, I called him on the way to the airport.

He missed my call, but rang me back when I was in Melbourne, the first stop on our trip. My mum, my sister and I were planning to head to his hometown the following week. I know what it sounds like – that I was flying halfway across the world to see the man who had been periodically ghosting me and repeatedly making me feel like a heartbroken fool – but I did have a real reason to be there. I was visiting my sister, remember? And while I could have easily avoided Dylan's particular city, I was also there for work, and my editor had specifically suggested I check out a cool hotel opening while I was that side of the world. I mean, who was I to go against her professional expertise?

At first the call with Dylan was friendly, but then he dropped the bombshell that he had started seeing someone, and he wanted me to know that if we were going to meet. Fate sure can be funny sometimes. He suggested breakfast.

I felt like I had been punched in the face, and I threw up from the anxiety of it all. I had dated other people, and I had gone long periods without thinking of him. But for some reason, there had always remained a seed of hope that if we could just be in the same place, the world would melt away again and we'd only have eyes for each other.

My mum and sister told me in no uncertain terms that I shouldn't go. I listened to them over the next few days, all the while pretending to consider cancelling. I always knew that I would go, though. It would have been too weird to be there after all that time and not; I didn't want to give myself a chance to regret anything or wonder 'What if?' I needed to leave that city knowing once and for all that what we had was done and gone.

He waited for me in the lobby of my hotel. The second I stepped into the elevator, it felt strangely familiar. I thought it was déjà vu, but then I remembered that night in Hong Kong. I'd been all nerves travelling up in a compact hotel elevator with him, and now, as we prepared to close our relationship once and for all, I was descending in one on my own, a bundle of nerves once again. But not the good kind.

'Hello, you.' He hugged me.

'Hi, hi,' I said, in a quieter voice than normal.

We walked to a café nearby, and as he took out his phone to pay for the drinks, I saw his background was a picture of him kissing his new girlfriend. When I tell you I nearly threw up again there and then, I wish it was because of the instant ick of witnessing someone with a snogging close-up as their phone background. Things that are equally gross include, but are not limited to: calling your partner 'Snugadoodle' in public; picking each other's pimples; and speaking to each other in a made-up language at a party. Instead, though, the nervous tummy was because, for a moment, I wished it was me in the picture.

It's obvious now that our relationship was over long before this moment, but sitting in that café, I wanted him and only him. I was looking for signs that he wasn't over me, either – that he regretted letting our chance pass us by.

We sat and ate. He devoured an egg in a brioche bun; it

made me queasy looking at him eating with such fervour as the yolk dribbled across his plate. It was grotesque. I picked at the banana bread in front of me. The conversation turned to his forty-fifth birthday, which he'd celebrated a few weeks earlier. Oh yes, this man was now a whopping forty-five years old. You might have thought he was in his late twenties based on his behaviour; indeed, I often forgot he was more than ten years older than me.

He told me he'd spent it in Cambodia with his girlfriend, mum and sister. My brain whirled like a slot machine, trying to make sense of the dates.

He went to the loo, which gave me a moment to collect myself. When he came back, I said, 'Sorry, I know it isn't really my business, but can I ask, when did you start seeing your girlfriend?'

He stared blankly at me. 'Oh. Is this because of the holiday?'

'Well, yes.' A pause. 'It wasn't that long ago you were telling me how lonely you were here, that you didn't fit in here – had you already started seeing her at that point? Because it's pretty weird if you had. Or was that just a lie?' I questioned.

He said that they had definitely started seeing each other *after* his last lengthy phone call to me: that gave them less than three months from first date to family holiday abroad. And that was at most. He wasn't sheepish or apologetic about it; he was trying to style it out as if that was totally normal. There was no way he would admit that he had lied to me, even though it would have been the decent thing to do.

'Okay,' I said.

'Okay,' he replied.

I knew this didn't make sense, that he was bending the truth at the very least – and probably had been for a long time. But I was more heartbroken by the realisation that he could have fallen for and committed to this other woman so quickly. He had introduced her to his family, gone on holiday, and become comfortable enough to refer to her so casually as his girlfriend.

Why, with me, had each of these steps seemed like huge, heavy milestones? What had I been lacking? I had blamed it on him. He was afraid of commitment. He was too obsessed with his job. He was a Peter Pan, still clinging to his youth. But here was proof that I just wasn't the right woman, at the right time and in the right place. This other woman was.

That's not to say I was absolving him of all guilt. Not in the slightest. He had kept me on hold for years, I'd never met his friends and he'd never met mine, and he was responsible for that. But I had thought it hadn't worked out between us because he didn't want a relationship. It turned out he did – just not with me. And I would never have been able to change that. I don't look back and wish I had been different, able to fit in with what he wanted. I do wish I had been different when it comes to how long I waited for him.

Before we left, I took my chance to tell him how I felt about the last three years. I had prepared for this with a note on my phone, like any self-respecting woman on the verge of a breakdown.

'Look, I need to say something; please let me say it all before you reply.' I looked him dead in the eye, determined not to let any tears escape.

The words didn't come out exactly as I wanted them to, but the general gist was there. I told him that he had used me as an emotional security blanket, knowing I would always reassure him. That so much of our relationship had been virtual, and he could no longer blame the pandemic for that. That he would pop up out of the blue and say big, bold things and then disappear again. That, eventually, he made me feel like I could never trust what he said.

He sat there nodding. At first, he tried to make it more light-hearted: 'Oh, I knew this conversation was coming. I'm ready, what else?' His words and the fact he was trying to make light of what had happened felt so disrespectful. I wanted to pummel him.

Eventually, he managed the minimal self-awareness needed to

realise from my steely expression that he wasn't going to be able to laugh his way out of the conversation. He turned serious. 'I always meant what I said in the moment.'

'Why did you meet me today?' I asked.

He laughed. 'I knew that if I didn't, I would lose you. That this would be the end.'

Even then, he was trying to maintain a hold over me. He wanted to keep this small ember burning in case he needed it to keep him warm in the future.

We said goodbye at the bus stop.

Only when I got back to my hotel room did I allow myself to sob. Dylan had disappeared on me so many times, and that was why he was so dangerous. He didn't have the courage to say goodbye and let me move on. And each time, I let myself dare to think that things would be different. I felt stupid for being so upset when it had been so long since we last went on a date, when we'd never even been a proper couple.

The time difference meant I couldn't call any friends back home, and I was too scared to tell my mum and sister what had happened. I thought they might say, *We told you so.* Both about that morning, and all the other times I had persisted with this man. They are better than my friends at telling things to me straight, and for the most part, I am grateful for that.

But when my mum entered the room, she could see how distraught I was, and she instantly comforted me. She reminded me that I finally had closure, and that was something to be thankful for. That it was okay to feel sad; I had believed in a future, and that imagined future was something I now needed to mourn. After a while she left and sent my sister in, knowing Kate could make me feel better simply with her presence. She'd probably say something silly that would draw me out of the sobs, if only for a moment. 'Have you ever thought about being a cow? Nothing to worry about, and you get to eat all day, straight from the floor. Like, imagine if the floor was made of pastrami . . .'

'Pastrami is made from beef, Kate. From cows.'

'Oh shit, yeah. Okay, not pastrami. Pizza. A floor made of pizza. Can't argue with that.'

For the next twenty-four hours, the skies were a new kind of grey. An Indian meal we ate tasted of nothing. I felt powerless and stupid. I had loved this man, and I knew now it really was over, before it had ever properly begun.

'At least I won't ever have to visit this hideous city again,' I said to my sister as we crossed the street on our final morning. 'Imagine, I could have ended up moving here one day and not been able to do anything about it.'

'Shh,' she said. 'The people around us probably live here, and you're insulting them purely because you're heartbroken.'

'I *am* heartbroken.'

'Why don't we try insulting Dylan instead? I can help. Honestly, I have lots of ideas. First off, his idea of a good time is a tacky circus-themed bar?? Or what about his terrible trousers?'

We left the city in a hire car, my mum, my sister and me. For them, it was like any other journey. For me, it was transformative. With each mile I put between myself and Dylan, I grew stronger. I knew I would never let someone hold this power over me again.

'Turn up the music, I love this song,' I said.

'Um, I was the one who introduced you to it – you don't have good enough taste,' Kate said, before singing along.

That night I felt properly hungry for the first time since we'd landed, and devoured a plateful of pasta. We shared a bottle of wine, and I could see my mum and sister watching me closely and carefully, not sure of my emotional state.

'I'm okay, really. I'm not going to burst into tears.'

'Thank god for that. I thought we might have to stage an intervention,' Kate said.

'I'll open another bottle.' My mum smiled.
'I love you both.'

I never regretted meeting Dylan for breakfast, even though it was painful. I knew for me it was the closure I needed to finally process what I had been through. Now, I try to remember that when I can't get that final chance to say goodbye, I can always find ways to create my own form of closure. Because the people who hurt you cannot heal you. Only you can do that. The breakfast had been a starting point; I did the rest of the hard work on my own.

Dylan returned to his favourite method of contact: emojis. A flame. Heart eyes.

I left him behind in Australia, and I haven't looked back.

Some things I've learned about getting over someone

♥ Getting under someone else actually does help (as long as it is not an ex).

♥ Getting drunk does *not* help – particularly if you're partial to a tipsy text.

♥ A one-way ticket or at the very least a solo holiday somewhere new is the best cure if you can make it work. Just ask Frances in *Under the Tuscan Sun*.

♥ You may find you've got a whole new set of hobbies: journaling, running and crying through romcoms.

♥ Bridget Jones had the right idea: a duvet and a pint of ice cream can solve all manner of heartbreaks.

♥ You must cut all contact for at least six months. It is the only way. Do not attempt immediately to stay friends.

♥ Learn from Elle Woods: if you need to win them back, they aren't worth it.

♥ This is not the time to choose a new hairstyle. And if you must do it, do not attempt to do it yourself.

♥ Something totally silly will eventually make you deep belly-laugh with friends again.

♥ If you try to rationalise ridiculous reasons for reaching out to them, you're not over them.

♥ If you check your Instagram story viewers for their name, you're not over them.

♥ If you message them to say Happy Christmas (or Happy Birthday, or Happy Any Holiday), you're not over them.

♥ If you say you're over them, you're not over them.

♥ One day, sooner than you think, you will get over them – and you won't even notice it's happened.

3

WHEN LIZZIE MET ZACK . . . AND LIAM

Starring the ones I had a threesome with

I never expected a weekend trip back to my university town to culminate in a threesome. I definitely wouldn't have guessed it would have been with two men I'd known for years. Nor that it would teach me a valuable lesson about casual sex. Later, when I was giving my friends the full rundown of what had happened, it helped that the two were in countless photos together on Facebook: 'They're cute, right?'

After graduating, I'd moved to London to try to get on the journalism career ladder. I'd started as an intern at a travel mag, and later managed to get a role that was part editorial and part admin assistant. I was living a life of extremes – one week I would be sent to the Maldives to drink champagne and eat freshly caught tuna from the sea, the next I couldn't afford anything other than beans on toast for dinner.

I was only twenty-three, but already overanalysing my life choices. I am type A and a serial overthinker. The job paid the bare minimum on the basis that there were quite a few perks, and I didn't know how long it would be before I could ask for a salary more in line with what my friends were earning. Sure, I got to stay in fancy places every six weeks or so, but that didn't make it any easier to pay my rent. It didn't help that most of my friends had gone down a more traditional route, securing coveted grad schemes with salaries that would grow exponentially – meanwhile, I was taping up boxes of magazines and answering reader complaints.

I also missed the spontaneity, camaraderie and sense of adventure that had anchored my university years. Now that we all had full-time jobs and lived in the far-out zones of the city, it wasn't possible to just pop over to a friend's place at a moment's notice. Nights out were less frequent and rarely with more than a pal or two. You wouldn't bump into half your course or halls in the random London pub you'd chosen. Hangovers were also now solitary hellish episodes rather than a pile of friends languishing on the sofa with mediocre pizza and reruns of our favourite shows. I hadn't bonded with my new housemates, two strangers whom I'd found on SpareRoom. We lived together, yes, but separately – retreating to our rooms as soon as we'd made dinner. I didn't even know their last names.

Funnily enough, one of those flatmates was actually the Hannah who I have mentioned several times, and is now one of my best friends, but when we first met she'd quite bluntly told me that she was planning on moving to Yorkshire so there wasn't time for us to become anything more than acquaintances. I was hurt by this, and so for the first year or so we weren't close. It was only when we both opened up about the men in our lives over drunk food in the kitchen one night that everything changed. We might not have ever had a friendship if it hadn't been for those heartbreaks. We laugh about that now.

All this is to say that that year, I felt a little lonely. My housemates were just housemates rather than friends, and my social life was a sliver of what it had been at university. So when I boarded the train, I was hoping for more than a reunion (I was visiting for the twenty-fifth anniversary of the student television station).

I wanted to feel young and spontaneous again. I wanted a story to laugh about the next day, like we'd always had when we were studying.

Back then, a night out wasn't a proper night out unless something fairly outrageous happened. Or at least outrageous in the eyes of a university student. Like the time my housemate stole the giant neon 'S' from a sign for the end-of-year ball because she thought it would look good in her room, or when a friend was found by an elderly couple sleeping on their sofa on a canal boat with no recollection of how he'd got there. Outrageous could also have meant anything to do with sex. Like when one friend was fingered by a guy she really fancied – on the entrance stairs to the club. Yes, there were cameras. Or when another got caught shagging her boyfriend in the bathroom stalls by a particularly unforgiving bouncer. They got kicked out and missed the DJ set they had been talking about for weeks. Or when I brought a close friend back after the grad ball, and my housemate stood in the corridor shouting up at us, 'Lizzie, what are you doing?? He's our brother! He's our *brother*!' Very distracting. But also very funny the next day. (In case of any confusion, he was not in any way related to either of us; my friend was just objecting to me getting sexy with one of our nearest and dearest friends.)

Once university was over, though, we'd transitioned to meeting for G&Ts after work and going home by 10pm.

I wanted to relish being part of something again, part of a group where friendships criss-crossed all over the room and everyone knew each other – and everything about each other. Luckily, that was just what was in store. Okay, so the actual celebration was a bit disappointing, but there was certainly going to be a story by morning.

If you want an idea of the first part of the night, think of a lacklustre wedding: an unmemorable three-course meal, cheesy music, and long speeches that seemed specifically designed to be ignored in a grand building on campus. I guess it was also the closest thing I've experienced to a high-school reunion like the ones you see in so many American films – in England, you'll only have one if you've got a double-barrelled name and went to a swanky school. I did not.

I was with two friends, Alice and Rebecca, whom I'd met back in my first year and have stayed close with ever since. We began with drinks at Rebecca's house, eager to catch up before we joined the others. Alice had a twisted ankle thanks to a trip to the Lake District wearing completely inappropriate shoes with a new boyfriend she was trying to impress, and Rebecca said she didn't fancy a Big Night Out. Not exactly the energy I had been hoping for on the train up.

Inside the hall, there was a collection of faces: some I recognised, some I didn't. Everyone had been involved with the student television station at some point over the last twenty-five years, though a significant proportion were from the last ten. I suppose it had been easier to contact those who had more recently graduated – or maybe it was because they, like me, weren't yet ready to say goodbye to the university lifestyle, so were far keener to trek back for the night.

As I scanned the room, there was one person I was on the lookout for: Connor. He was three years older than me, and I'd had a crush on him from pretty much the first moment I met him. He had this playful energy that was infectious. Whenever he was fooling around, telling a joke, setting up a game, you wanted to be part of it. Or at least I did.

I was chatting to another friend, Zack, although I wasn't really listening. I was doing a good job of seeming engaged, nodding my head and laughing at the right moments, all the while watching Connor out of the corner of my eye. I wondered when he would come over to say hello.

Over the year our paths crossed at university, Connor and I had spent lots of time together filming and messing around.

We'd also see each other most weeks at house parties, which were always more fun with him.

I'd never told anyone, even my closest friends, that I liked him, because he had a girlfriend. I didn't think my feelings were requited in any way and it felt pointless to voice them. I thought perhaps he saw me as a younger sister figure due to our age gap – it was only a few years, but at university that can feel monumental.

I'd only realised I might have been wrong about his feelings for me on the final night we had spent together before he graduated. Frankly, our behaviour that evening bordered on inappropriate, given his relationship status. I blame the overwhelming, all-consuming feeling of 'one last chance' in the air.

Let's flashback to several years previously . . .

It was the annual television society gala: the tradition was to go to a rooftop bar with bottomless booze and give out awards for the best actor and best actress of the year. There had been soap operas, dramas, sitcoms and more. People took it extremely seriously. If you lingered too long in the loos later on in the night, you'd probably hear someone bitching about how the wrong person had won. Or how they had only got cast in that part in the first place because the director had fancied them and thought it would help their chances of getting laid. Yes, it was melodramatic, but then again we were in a television society full of larger-than-life personalities. It was incestuous. Everyone ostensibly hated it, but secretly loved it.

At one point, a mutual friend commented on the fact I was wearing Connor's jacket. I'd been cold, and he'd handed it to me without saying anything before striding off. It was loud, and I couldn't hear the friend properly. But I could have sworn he said, 'You know he's always had a thing for you, right?'

Obviously, the first thing I did was run to find Alice because I needed her interpretation of the conversation. Plus, I wanted further external validation that the guy I'd been into for a whole year had potentially felt the same the entire time.

She let out a tipsy squeal: 'I knew he did. And you like him too, right?'

'How do you know?' I asked.

'Oh come on, everyone knows,' she replied, dashing my hopes that my year-long performance of 'nonchalant cool girl' had been Oscar-worthy. No wonder I didn't win best actress.

After midnight, Connor and I began to flirt unashamedly. At one point he held my hand for a few seconds too long. At another, I playfully ruffled his hair. It was clear that our attraction was mutual, and we were showing it in a way it had never been expressed before. I think it was something about the night being his last hurrah: there was a feeling of now or never.

And yet he still had the girlfriend, so I knew deep down it wouldn't and couldn't turn into anything more. There would be no kiss, as that would cross a line we couldn't come back from. So instead we eked out the night, neither of us wanting to leave. We went to a club and then a house party, where we massively overstayed our welcome. The hosts clearly wanted to go to bed, tidying around us and yawning loudly. I didn't want to leave knowing the spell of that one last night would break when the sun rose in the morning.

We left at gone 6am, and two good mutual friends were waiting on my street to ensure we went our separate ways. I believe we would have anyway, but it helped that they were there.

A few days later, I got a call from Connor – and to this day, it's one of the most awkward phone calls I've ever received. Incidentally, it was also the last time I would speak to him before the reunion years later. I had just uploaded a Facebook album of, let's say, 200 photos from the night out, as was the way back then. Several of my friends would have also done the same. Each album had a title like 'WE ARE ON A ROOFTOP MOTHERFUCKERS' or 'WHO STOLE MY SHOE?? BEST

NIGHT EVER'. Suddenly, my phone began to ring. I hadn't expected to hear from him again.

'Hello?'

'Oh hi, Lizzie. How are you? Are you back home now?' His voice sounded nervous, which I wasn't used to.

'No, I'm still here. What about you?'

'Yeah, just packing up my stuff.'

'Okay.' A long pause. 'Connor, why are you calling me?'

And then he spoke so quickly it took me a second to comprehend what he was saying. 'Um, okay, this is really awkward, but you know that album you just uploaded to Facebook? Well, there's a picture in it of us kissing and I'm worried my girlfriend is going to see it. I need you to take it down. Please take it down.'

I was gobsmacked. We hadn't kissed. What on earth was he talking about? 'Umm, what?' I asked.

'Oh my god. Fred has just commented on it. Fred has just commented saying, "Oh dear." You need to take this down now.' His voice got squeakier and squeakier.

Sure enough, a little number one had appeared over the notifications icon on my Facebook homepage. I clicked on it to see Fred's comment. I laughed out loud.

'Lizzie,' screeched Connor.

'Connor,' I said in between laughter. 'The reason Fred has commented on this picture is because it is a picture of *Fred* and me kissing.' Fred and I had thought it would be funny to take a series of snogging photos after a number of Jägerbombs. Fred was a close friend of mine at the time, and not remotely interested in women. The others had cheered us on; the more dramatic we were, the better.

'What?' Connor was in disbelief. 'Oh, oh.' They had both been wearing suits and had a similar haircut. But the fact Connor hadn't recognised it wasn't him when I clearly could was quite hilarious.

'Did you think we had kissed? Because we didn't kiss,' I said.

'Of course not. Sorry to have bothered you. I've really got to go, so . . . Have a good summer. Goodbye.' He hung up.

Without hesitation, I called Alice to tell her every detail. I've always found it incredible how a five-minute interaction with a boy can be dissected and laughed about and re-evaluated and reimagined with your friends for the best part of an hour. Who am I kidding? Two hours. At least.

So, back to the reunion . . .

There I was, knowing I would be seeing Connor again for the first time after several years. I couldn't help but feel a bit nervous and wonder whether there would still be the same energy between us. Maybe, just maybe, he and the girlfriend would have drifted apart. I wanted to not be attracted to him any longer, to not be bothered if he was there.

When we did finally speak, his situation was the same. It was disappointing even though I'd expected it. He was in one of those perfectly matched couples that people fawn over, and yet I'd held on to the secret hope that post-uni life had revealed some cracks in their foundations, and this might be our time instead. What if he was 'the one' for me, but he'd already met his 'the one'? Was this some flaw in the matrix? I felt sentimental about seeing him again, but our chemistry was subdued. Somehow, the fact we were now adults with jobs in the real world not only made his relationship seem more serious, but it also made our coy chit-chat feel childlike.

I decided to go and speak to someone else; nothing good would come from another night of flirting with Connor. I found Liam, who I'd not seen in years. He was a good distraction.

Later, taxis arrived en masse and we hurtled towards the city centre for an after-party. Alice had decided to head home (the pain of the ankle had become too much; plus I had a feeling she wanted to make a soppy phone call to her new love interest) so it was just me and Rebecca. The location was odd. Ping-pong tables filled the space, leaving no room for dancing or mingling. Lots of static conversations took place in cramped corners, and the evening never really got off the ground. We had the same chat on repeat: 'Where do you live now? What do you do? Do you still do any acting or presenting?'

Many of the friendships we'd thought would last forever had faltered without something as concrete as a film studio to bind us together. And although for me it had only been one short year since we'd left university, it felt like a decade.

When the evening's celebrations came to an end at not much past midnight, I was disenchanted. There'd been no silly behaviour, no ridiculous stories to recount the next day – there hadn't even been any dancing. Where were the rounds of shots? Where was the person spinning on a kitchen table in their knickers, throwing glitter in the air? Where was the moment where two unexpected people would kiss, and we'd all cheer before they snuck upstairs? Instead we'd sat around tables (apparently too old for standing), having conversations that were marginally better than the 'dull and disinteresting' variety. I felt old before my time.

I said this to Rebecca as we climbed the steep street to her house where we were both staying, convinced that was it. The Big Night Out had not materialised and now it never would. We couldn't hope for anything more. Then I felt my phone vibrate in my bag, and a smile spread across my face. I stopped. Maybe the night wasn't over just yet. For a split second, I wondered if it was Connor.

It was a message from an unknown number:

> Where did you go?

It was a question full of possibility. Rebecca peered over my shoulder.

I fired back:

Sorry, who is this?

It's Zack. I'm with Liam.

Interesting. Not who I had expected, but slowly it started to make sense. They knew Rebecca and I were together. And Zack had told me over dinner that he thought Rebecca was intriguing, which I'd already let her know. Come to think of it, Liam had been quite flirty with me earlier. This was good news, at least in my opinion.

I'd seen Liam in arty films on the student television channel during university, and thought he was talented and rugged and cool. I still did.

Zack was a closer friend, but I'd never been attracted to him, and knew he hadn't been into me either. It was one of those perfectly platonic friendships, and I would have recommended him to any of my single pals. He was sweet and charming.

Another message came through.

Do you want to go for another drink, us four?

I turned to Rebecca with the excitement of someone who had just won the lottery: 'What do you think? Let's go!' I started skipping. This was what I'd been wanting all evening: a night out that wasn't just another night out.

I could tell straight away she wasn't up for it. We reached her house and started making bagels in our pyjamas. I kept texting the boys back, not ready to give up yet, even though the cream cheese on my chin said otherwise.

I tried one last time: 'Come on, Rebecca, let's be young and wild and free,' I said, half-joking. 'What else are we going to do? Go to sleep?' I didn't want the opportunity to pass us by, to slide into bed after another less-than-exciting evening to wonder about what might have happened if we'd seized the moment just a little more.

'Sorry, Lizzie, I'm just not feeling it,' she replied. 'Why don't you go on your own?'

I knew there was another reason Rebecca was feeling hesitant: she hadn't slept with anyone yet. I asked if this was holding her back and, from her forced smile, I knew it was. It was something we had talked about at length during our friendship. She wanted to have sex, and at the same time she didn't want to do it for the first time with just anyone. She wanted her first time to be special, just like I had, just like so many people wish for it to be.

This pressure for the first time to be particularly momentous, though, means that it rarely is. A straw poll of my friends shows that in most cases it was either a) painful, b) awkward or c) a mix of the first two.

'I don't want to go, and have them assume we are going to have sex. And then I'll have to explain why I don't want to,' she said.

'Okay, first of all, you never ever have to have sex with someone, no matter the situation. You can always say no. And secondly, you never have to explain why you don't want to,' I replied.

'I know, but I'd rather just not go,' Rebecca said.

I knew where she was coming from, and also knew that these feelings had complicated her university experience, and were still doing so now. I absolutely didn't want to push her into anything she wasn't comfortable with.

'I get it,' I answered.

'You can still go though; I'll just be asleep here,' she said.

'I can't go on my own.' I shook my head and laughed at the idea. 'What if they think I want a threesome? It would be so weird.'

'It's only weird if you make it weird. I think you should go; you and Liam will probably peel off,' Rebecca countered. 'You want to go, and you don't have to do anything you don't want to. Like you just said. Go and see. Be spontaneous for the both of us.'

I hesitated, thinking through what she'd said. Rebecca was

right; if I didn't go, I was ignoring my own advice. Moments earlier, I'd thought it was absurd to leave the flat on my own, but I knew I wanted to go even if I only ended up being out for an extra hour. I told the boys Rebecca was going to bed, but I was still wide awake. They told me it was getting late, so to come if I was coming. I said okay. All the bars had closed, though, so we'd have to have a drink in their hotel room, came the reply. This was escalating rapidly. I ordered an Uber before I could overthink this new development, had a quick shower and threw my dress back on.

Rebecca said, 'You look hot.'

I appreciated the fact she knew exactly what I needed: to be hyped up.

Outside, the car was not there and the waiting time kept increasing. It was already 4am. I was beginning to think it might be a sign, but then a silver Prius appeared around the corner and I decided that if the tiniest part of me wanted to go, I should.

My phone vibrated again in the car.

The message read:

> Okay, we couldn't find any alcohol, but we can offer you a peppermint tea when you get here

Zack and Liam were staying at the Marriott. I rang the buzzer when I arrived to be let in, as it was well past normal hours, and the concierge asked for the name. I realised I had no idea which of them had booked it. I took a punt: 'Cooke?' The doors slid apart. I avoided eye contact and walked purposefully to the lift.

But when I reached the second-floor hallway, panic struck me again. I took two steps forward, then two steps back. I shook my head and strode forward. Only to spin around 180 degrees and stare back at the exit. And repeat. If someone had watched the footage back on CCTV, I'm sure a vintage Dido song would have been the perfect accompaniment. But rather than deciding whether or not to confront Keira Knightley about my true feelings for her, I was debating whether I was cool enough to have a threesome.

I'd joked about it at Rebecca's, but now that I was here, it did seem somewhat likely. Did I really want to have a threesome? And even if I did, did I want it to be with two people I knew so well? What if they were both just sitting there, naked except for their bow ties, waiting for me? Would I suddenly get the ick? Or would I be turned on? How would I ever look at them again?

I was in front of the door by now. I took a deep breath and let out a silent squeal – and then knocked sharply three times before I could change my mind. Footsteps approached. The door swung open. Zack was in front me, and I could see Liam smiling from inside the room, both still in their suits from the evening. Was that disappointment I felt?

'Hellooo, come on in,' they said, almost in unison. My own 'Hello' back was bubbling over with nervous energy, three decibels higher than what could have been considered nonchalant. Oh well, I've never been nonchalant. I've learned to lean into that now.

I followed Zack and sat down on the bed next to him, but not touching him. Liam was facing us from a chair. He looked just as handsome as he had earlier. Had they decided to sit like this, or was it by chance? I would have thought that if they'd planned it, they'd be sitting the other way round. It was Liam who fancied me, not Zack. Still, I couldn't help but be aware of Zack's every movement, thinking with each shift that he might make a move. But it didn't come.

'One cup of peppermint tea, I believe?' said Zack.

'Yes please, apparently it's the "in" drink nowadays,' I replied.

'We did try to find a bar, but it's not London, you know. Everything closes very early,' joked Liam. He flipped the switch on the kettle behind him.

We all pretended this was completely normal, as if it was 4pm and not 4am. As if we regularly hung out, the three of us, drinking mugs of peppermint tea. As if there was no tension in the air. I tried to look deep into their eyes to see what they were thinking, but neither gave anything away.

And so we chatted for at least an hour, falling back on topics that were easy: mainly the mutual friends we still saw, and recounting lore from our university days.

'Are Amir and Olivia still together? As if they kissed for the first time after presenting the big hockey match and someone caught it on camera.'

'Whatever happened to Seamus? Someone told me he moved to Mexico and became a yoga teacher.'

We had all heard and told these stories many times. The conversation was nothing new, but there was an undercurrent of something else. If I could feel it, then surely they could too?

'When did everyone else get so boring?' asked Zack. 'They all went home so early.'

Liam and I agreed. The subtext was: *We aren't boring, that's why we're here.* We were still capable of being fun. We were spontaneous people. The kind of people that might, I don't know, have a threesome on a whim?

It was only then that Zack finally put his arm around me and stroked my hair. I stared into my mug of tea, not wanting to make eye contact with him or Liam. I thought if I did, I might burst into laughter, and that might come across as if I was uncomfortable. I wasn't. I just couldn't quite understand how we had got here. The room was brightly lit and it didn't feel conducive to setting the mood. Still, my stomach was doing somersaults and my body had started to tingle.

I had never seen Zack like this. He was a friend and nothing more. I'd never wanted to snog him, let alone slip into bed with him. But from the moment I'd stepped in the room that night, it had been different. Even the way his eyes looked was inconsistent with how I pictured them. Had they always been that colour?

Not long after, we decided it was time for bed. Liam came over and we got under the covers, and he switched off the lamp. Darkness. We were all still fully clothed. Me in a nice dress, the boys in posh shirts.

'Goodnight.'

'Goodnight.'

'Goodnight.'

We lay there together, our sides touching – it was the smallest double bed I'd ever seen – and the silence hung in the air.

For a moment, I worried that the night was truly over. And that was when I knew what I really wanted: I had a deep desire to be completely consumed by these two men. I was crushed at the thought of us falling asleep in a row, dreaming nothing but sweet, innocent dreams. But none of us were drunk. We were all just friends. Maybe I had imagined the sexual tension in my head.

Then it was as if a wave crashed over me – first Zack rolled on to his side and pulled my head closer to kiss me. It was a long, salty smooch, and from behind me I felt Liam's hand ripple up my leg until he reached my inner thigh. I wanted him to keep going but he stopped abruptly, moving his hand to my shoulder to pull me over to his side of the bed and kiss me too.

Zack began to unbutton my dress – there was a long line of buttons up the back – and when he was done, the two of them peeled it off. I tugged at their trousers, and they pulled them down and off too. The three of us knelt in the centre of the bed – it strangely felt almost ceremonial – hands moving across each other's bodies for a while. Then we fell flat, and shifted round and round. A soundtrack of moans and groans. It felt natural, easy. When I remember this moment, I can see how confident I felt, how empowered I was. Not to mention, I felt sexier than I had ever felt before.

A slew of romcoms in the early 2010s, in particular *Friends with Benefits* and *No Strings Attached*, had been instrumental in showing me that casual sex could be liberating. That women could enjoy it and want it just as much as men. It wasn't something to feel bad about. Going after what you want, eschewing the role of the damsel in distress, can be very, very sexy. (Let's just forget the part where the main characters inevitably end up lovesick and together after all.)

There were awkward moments, too, of course. Like when Zack tried to take off my bra and struggled for a few moments too long. Liam went to help and Zack told him curtly, 'I can do it, give me a second.'

'All right, mate.' Liam backed off.

At one point, I did end up laughing, and we had to stop for a moment. I asked, 'If someone had said on the train up here that this would happen, would you have believed them?'

The boys said absolutely not – and then we were kissing and fooling around again. Later, we fell asleep like three spoons.

When an alarm jolted us awake, I was surprised that I didn't feel awkward lying naked between the two of them. We spent the morning drifting in and out of sleep, hands on bums and boobs.

'I was thinking – let's not tell anyone about this,' Zack mumbled.

'Fine by me,' I replied. 'Was that your first threesome?'

'Yes,' said Zack.

'No, not even close,' said Liam.

Zack and I rolled our eyes.

I returned to Rebecca's and we met Alice for brunch. Of course, I didn't count either of them as part of the group of people we wouldn't tell. Rebecca had known I had gone there at 4am, duh. She wasn't going to accept that we had a cup of peppermint tea and fell asleep. Alice had no idea, having left hours before, but she was one of my best friends. As we perused the menu, I told her I'd had a threesome the night before – but could she guess who it was with? It was unexpected, sure, but the fact we knew these men so well and had spent countless nights out with them previously made it funnier. And as she spat out different names, we all laughed. When she guessed Connor, with a solemn face, I was glad I could say no. When she finally guessed the correct two, we were crying with laughter again. 'Zack and Liam?! Together?!'

I enjoyed giving a dramatic retelling of the night's events, how it had happened and what it had been like when I'd first walked in the room, and then later what they were like in bed. Naturally, Alice and Rebecca asked who was better. 'They were different,' I replied like a politician, before confessing. I do apologise to anyone who was quietly trying to eat poached eggs on toast that day: our high-pitched screams were uncontrollable. Question after question was thrown at me. At one point I said, 'I felt like the star of the show' – then nearly died of embarrassment. Alice won't let me forget that line even now.

It's nearly a decade later, and I can confidently say that night was the best casual sex I've ever had. The very nature of the dynamic meant it was impossible to get caught up in emotions. Impossible to read the situation wrong. I knew it would never happen again, and so did Liam and Zack.

On the train home, I didn't anxiously await a text. I didn't wonder if I'd see them again. I didn't overthink what I'd done or said. I didn't have something in the pit of my stomach telling me I'd been too vulnerable too early. I didn't check their WhatsApps to see when they were last online. It was a freeing feeling.

I'd like to say that I applied this thinking to future non-casual scenarios, knowing how much better it is to let things be without analysing every possible scenario. I'd like to say I never again checked the read receipts from a recent flame and talked at length with a friend about what it might mean. I'd like to say my anxious attachment style disappeared into thin air.

Of course, that's not what happened. The parameters of a three-some and a fledgling relationship are completely different, and it would be cruel to expect my mind to behave in the same way for both. But I did begin to inch towards this healthier attitude.

As for Rebecca? Her first time was right for her when it

happened. In fact, it was probably better than most people's first experience. She knew what she wanted and she got it.

And as predicted, nothing ever happened again with Liam or Zack, or both of them. I did bump into each of them a few times, out in Brixton, at a friend's birthday, having lunch with my dad. Yes, that was awkward, and no, I don't know why I told my dad I'd had a threesome with Zack when he asked how we knew each other. It turns out that was a step too far in the oversharing department. Sorry, Dad.

Liam even popped up on my LinkedIn one time a few years later. I connected with him, and the website prompted me with the question: 'What skills would you recommend Liam for?'

I clicked 'Teamwork'. It seemed apt.

Some things I've learned about sex

- ♥ Ignore Carrie Bradshaw and her three-date rule. It really doesn't matter when you sleep with them. Do what feels right.

- ♥ The problem with spending money on lingerie is that most men just want to rip it off the second they see it.

- ♥ Long-distance will allow you to perfect the art of the nude.

- ♥ There are certain techniques that will become like folklore among your friends. Read: The Glug Glug 3000.

- ♥ The Bermondsey tennis courts are surprisingly well suited to al fresco fun in central London.

- ❤ Talking about condoms is never sexy, but don't let that be a reason not to.

- ❤ Everyone has a fantasy, even if they don't know it yet. (Ahem, the piano scene in *Pretty Woman*.)

- ❤ There is no Google Map to your clit. You may have to provide instructions.

- ❤ You should never fake an orgasm – unless you're proving a point, like in *When Harry Met Sally*.

- ❤ Hostels almost always have somewhere private if you know where to look.

- ❤ Know what you want and what you like, and tell them.

- ❤ Wear the trench coat with nothing underneath.

- ❤ Sometimes it just doesn't work, and you can't force it.

- ❤ When it *does* work, it's pure magic. Don't settle for less than magic.

4

TO THE BOY I LOVED BEFORE

Starring the one who was my first love

Sometimes I wish I could replicate the fiery feeling of teenage love: that ravenous desire that feels so all-consuming you might just explode. But I know it's impossible. Because no one else will be the first. Because the growing flames of heady teen hormones are the secret ingredient.

Ezra was that explosive crush for me. I met him on my very first day at a new school, aged fifteen, and I was immediately drawn to him. He was different from any of the other boys I'd met before, which was not too much of a surprise given I'd moved from the suburbs of San Francisco to Swindon.

But you don't have to move to another country to know exactly what I am talking about. It's the kind of feeling you really only get once. When you can't think about anything else but the possibility of kissing them when they are in the room (okay, also when they're not in the room); when your body vibrates when someone says their name. When you are absolute in your belief that this person is completely perfect and everyone else is so stupid for not seeing it. When you feel like no one else could possibly understand what you're feeling, no one else could have ever loved in this way before. Teenagers have a tendency to think they are right about absolutely everything, and romance is no exception.

Up until this point I'd had many crushes, but none of them had materialised into anything and I hadn't even come close to a first kiss. Whenever the conversation at a sleepover turned to boys, I would go pink in the face and be too embarrassed to admit who I really liked. It made me feel too vulnerable.

I hadn't been a nerd in America, but I'd definitely stood out as quirky in what was a very mainstream suburban school. It was the kind of place you would have seen in countless teenage movies, many of which were, of course, set in California, just like my school: easy-to-spot cliques in the courtyard, Friday-night football games with some unlucky kid in the mascot costume, jerk jocks with cool cars in the parking lot, groups gossiping in locker-filled hallways, that sort of thing.

I wore a Kooks band T-shirt on repeat instead of the unofficial Abercrombie & Fitch uniform (I didn't even own a pair of jeans). I hadn't experimented with make-up yet, although everyone else seemed to, and I was the palest in my friendship group by a country mile as I spent the long summers visiting my mum across the pond rather than hanging out by one of the many pools in town.

Boy-frenzy would reach a pinnacle each time a school dance rolled around. At least twice a year we would gather in the gymnasium, large groups of girls on one side and guys on the other. The chosen few would meet in the middle for a slow dance, arms locked rigid to keep distance between them, while the rest of us stood on the sidelines giggling. I never ventured into the centre because it felt terrifying.

In high school, which I only experienced for a year before moving to England, things changed overnight. You went from being the oldest in a school of ten- to thirteen-year-olds, to suddenly the youngest, sharing the halls with eighteen-year-olds. These were not boys and girls – they were men and women. Or at least it felt that way. The first dance, Homecoming, took me by complete surprise. I didn't have older siblings or older friends, so I didn't know what to expect. I'd anticipated more of the chaste gymnasium routine. How wrong I was. My first clue should have been what my friends were wearing: no one wanted to look cute anymore, they wanted to look sexy. Everyone else seemed to have got the memo except me.

Instead of two separate groups, there was just a huge mosh pit of teens, and the new dance move to repeat was what we called 'freaking'. Or, as my friend whispered in my ear when I asked what everyone was doing – 'fucking with clothes on'. Parent chaperones did their best to move between the crowd and peel young, sweaty bodies apart, but it was an impossible task. There were far more horny teens than parents, and almost as soon as they had been pulled apart, they were humping each other again. It was like a mating scene in a David Attenborough documentary. I felt miles out of my comfort zone, and so I hated it.

For the next school dance, I conspired with my dad and pre-tended he had grounded me for some made-up reason so I didn't have to go again. He played his part well, repeating his rehearsed lines in front of my friends. I knew then he would do whatever it took to protect me and help me feel better. He had encouraged me to try going again initially, but when he saw the tears welling in my eyes, he took me at my word.

It's strange for me now to remember the younger version of myself saying no to things out of fear. As someone who saw social situations as stressful and to be avoided. Someone who decided it was better not to go to something if there was a risk of poten-tial embarrassment – particularly when there were boys. I know everyone thinks they were awkward as a young teen, but I really was. I didn't have enough confidence, I didn't think I was pretty in the same way as my friends, and I put too much emphasis on male attention equating to self-worth. When friends got asked to school dances and I didn't, I thought there must be something wrong with me. After all, the happily ever after of a romcom didn't exist if the main character didn't end up locking lips at the altar with the love of her life, an industrial fan just out of shot, wafting her perfect hair. This pernicious message was everywhere, so it's not a surprise it had become so ingrained and impacted my own self-esteem. Even now, it's rare for a romcom to end with the heroine on her own.

When I moved continents, I decided it was time for a reset. It was the perfect opportunity. I didn't want to be the quirky girl anymore. I wanted boys to like me. I was still by no means a cool girl – I never will be (nor do I want to be any longer) – but I did start wearing lip gloss and straightening my hair. I mean, that's all it takes for Mia in *Princess Diaries*, right? The glow-up scene is a mainstay of the genre, with a montage of fabulous, fun outfits alongside new hair and make-up – and, of course, a ceremonial crunch when the hideous glasses are finally snapped. It's a ridiculous premise, though, that a new miniskirt and contacts can instantly make you irresistible, and a very shallow, mainstream idea of what makes a person attractive. Not to mention the most dangerous message of the whole thing: that you can't just be yourself if you want a guy to like you.

Ezra was part of the new friendship group I'd formed, and I'd look forward to lunchbreaks when I could flirt with him. I could sense him flirting back. It was a new feeling to be liked in return and I was terrified I had got it all wrong. What if he was simply making fun of me and I was too stupid to see it?

Of course, online we would flirt even more. This was the heyday of MSN, when you'd race home and quickly boot up your computer to message your crush. Ezra's status was always some cryptic, depressing song lyric. Other boys messaged me – proof that I'd been successful in my efforts to transform into someone fanciable – but I was never that interested. I was on MSN for one purpose and one purpose only, to see the magic words: 'Eeeezrageezer93 is online'. If he didn't message first, I'd go offline and online again multiple times to try to get his attention. Most times, it worked.

Ezra wasn't an emo kid. He had longish black hair that he straightened meticulously each morning; he was the drummer in a band with his friends, and they'd play local gigs; he had a strangely dark sense of humour. Okay, maybe he was an emo kid.

Either way, he was an enigma, and I wanted to solve him. I paid attention to comments he made and started listening to the same alternative music as him, reading the same dystopian books as him, hoping this would make him like me more, or at least take notice of me. I'd stay up way past my bedtime, messaging him until the early hours. My mum had no idea – I'd let her say good-night and turn out the lights, but as soon as the door clicked shut, I'd pull out my laptop from under the duvet, the screen glowing in the darkness. I thought our chats were deep and complex; it wasn't just a line or two about our school days, we'd often send chunky paragraphs debating the intricacies of a particular meaty topic. Drugs, religion, politics, you name it. To the teenage me, it was proof we connected on a deeper level. That he was interested in what I had to say, and perhaps in turn, interested in me.

It was eighteen months before we officially became an item, though the flirting never stopped and my crush on him never waned. I did fancy other boys, but my feelings for Ezra were always deeper. We started to see each other more outside of school, always in a group setting. Friends would take it in turns to host a sleepover, and ten or so of us would stay up late watching films and playing stupid pranks. If we were lucky, someone's older sibling might sneak us a few hideously blue WKDs, and we'd take a picture of our dyed tongues as proof of how 'grown-up' we were. Ezra would play-fight with me, jumping from the sofa to bear-hug me to the floor – it was a happy accident that we would then end up next to each other when it was time to go to bed, under one duvet.

At first, that was all it was. The two of us sleeping beneath the same blanket. But soon we began to sneak our heads under for a kiss. Things would get more heated, in a teenage kind of way, with us trying to make as little noise as possible when all I wanted was to scream out with joy. I cringe now at the thought there were so many other people sleeping (or trying to) in the same room.

I began spending literal hours getting ready for social events where there was a chance this would happen. I would shave every inch of my body in the shower, and then again in the bath just to be sure I hadn't missed a single hair. Afterwards, I'd apply layer after layer of scented moisturiser in every nook and cranny. I was meticulous; I was as slippery as a seal.

Each time we fooled around, I thought that something was about to change. That he would tell me he liked me; that he would become my boyfriend. That was the order of things, that was what was supposed to happen (okay, minus the heavy petting). Not so. I had watched this play out on screen so many times. Boy meets girl, they kiss and fall in love, they live happily ever after. They don't go to third base before an actual date. I knew exactly how Mia felt in *Princess Diaries* when she didn't get her foot-pop moment for her first kiss. I felt guilty; I felt less than good enough.

The first few times after we'd fooled around, we didn't acknowledge it had happened. Our MSN chats stayed the same; our lunchtime flirts continued. I kept thinking he would say something, but when he didn't it felt as if I had imagined it all. It was agonising not knowing whether our sleepover antics meant anything, whether he actually liked me. This was the only reason I finally had the courage to ask: 'What is this?' I wasn't brave, I was exasperated. He shut me down. Told me that he wasn't looking to be in a relationship.

'I'm never going to be your knight in shining armour. I'm telling you now to never expect that from me.' This man (I mean, boy) was sixteen when he said this. If that's not proof of how over-wrought we all are as teenagers, then I don't know what is. I never asked for a knight, or a prince, just someone who would like and respect me. I felt like I was asking too much.

He'd had other girlfriends – at the pivotal ages of thirteen and fourteen – but they'd made him recognise commitment wasn't what he wanted. He was a lone wolf. I wasn't going to change that. It sounds so ridiculous now, but at the time I thought it was all so serious, particularly as I felt like he was so much more experienced than me. And I don't think it was an excuse on his part; I think he honestly believed he was completely unsuited for love, in the dramatic way only a teenager can. With distance, I also wonder if his behaviour said less about him and more about the unfair pressure placed on young boys – just as much as young girls – to assume preset 'roles'. He was a teen with a limited pool of romance role models, just as I was.

Still, I pleaded with him to try. His answer was a flat-out no. The fact that he didn't want us to be together made me feel like there was something lacking in me. A sense, unfortunately, that became so hardwired I went on to wonder the same in other relationships. Maybe I wasn't as pretty as the other girls he had dated? Maybe I wasn't as fun? Maybe I wasn't as funny? There had to be a reason – and the reason had to be me. I cried. And I cried. And I cried some more. There wasn't a single sofa cushion or pillow in my house that hadn't soaked up my teenage angst tears. Looking back, I'm sad for the sixteen-year-old me – not because she cried, but because her self-esteem was so low. I wish I could squeeze her and tell her to believe in herself.

After these crescendos, we'd have a week or so where we wouldn't chat as much, but then he'd pick up the conversation again. I was always so relieved when he did. Things would go back to normal, and before I knew it we'd be under the covers once more. Kissing him was electric, but it was always in secret, always something others weren't allowed to know about. And the conversation that followed was always the same. I was constantly confused and hurt, flip-flopping from pure joy and excitement to deep distress. I was consumed by him.

In a diary I kept at the time, I didn't even have the words

to describe what was happening. All I wrote was, 'It happened again.' I told myself I didn't include the details in case my mum went snooping, but really it was because I felt ashamed. Why did I keep letting it continue when I knew there was little hope that things might change? Why did I let him take what he wanted without meeting me halfway? I think part of it was because movies had taught me that sometimes men take longer to understand what they want. You just had to wait.

My friend Chris was one of the only ones who knew anything had happened between me and Ezra. He saw me fall apart countless times, but never made me feel stupid. It must have been exhausting for him to see the roller coaster I was on, particularly when he mainly saw the lows. When things were good, I didn't need his help.

Then a funny thing happened. Just as I finally came to terms with the fact that Ezra and I would never be a couple, he changed his mind, just like the romcoms had told me he would. I'd been on a few dates with someone I'd met outside of school; we'd been to the cinema and to the circus. And I noticed that Ezra had started to get – no – could it be – jealous? Then, at my birthday lunch with friends, a boy I had no interest in gave me a hideously misjudged teddy bear holding a heart as a present. If this had been a movie, the camera would have panned past the general merriment to reveal Ezra at the end of the table, fists clenched and seething.

We started to hang out just the two of us, which we'd never done before, and then one day, he asked: 'Do you want to be my girlfriend?' It seemed so out of the blue, but that didn't matter; I felt euphoric. Everything had slotted into place – although in the first days of our relationship, I kept looking at him as if he would suddenly disappear and I'd realise it was all a dream.

We celebrated each tiny milestone: a week as boyfriend and girlfriend, a month, two. When he posted on my Facebook wall calling me his personal nickname with a million xs for all to see, I couldn't stop smiling. Social media validation equalled 'true love'.

Much later on, he told me it was while we were watching *500 Days of Summer* that he'd decided he wanted to be together. Or at the very least, give it a go. It was one of the first of a new generation of cool romcoms, an anti-romcom if you will. It's whimsical and light-hearted, yes, but it's also a much more realistic take on love, the key point being that the main characters do not end up together. I couldn't understand why this had been the catalyst for him. He never really explained it to me, but now I suppose it was because it removed the pressure of a happy ending. If you felt something, you could try it, and if it didn't work out, it wasn't the end of the world. There were no villains.

And once we were together, it was easy to don rose-tinted glasses and wipe our particularly tear-stained history from the memory bank. Because from then on, Ezra was unconditional in his love for me. He said those three words a few months in, in a quiet and calm voice, as we sat on his bed and he looked into my eyes, and I felt my heart implode. I squeezed his hands back and whispered, 'I love you too.' We kept saying it back and forth, getting louder and louder. We couldn't get enough of those words. They were insufficient to describe how we felt. He made me feel the highest of highs; he showed me he loved me again and again.

Yes, it was teenage love, and that holds a huge power in itself, because it's the first time you've experienced many of these feelings. The first time you've said you're in love. The first time you've kissed someone, the first time you've felt really turned on, the first time you've wanted someone to touch every single part of your body. But even now, I don't like to call it that; it sounds so trivial, a category of love that is lesser-than. And I don't think it was lesser-than; it was powerful and proud and formative. I was not the same girl after I fell in love with him, and I don't think he was the same boy.

I can remember feeling like Allie in *The Notebook* during her first summer with Noah, flushed and heady with love; like Bella in *Twilight*, a misfit (like me) who'd moved to a new town (like me) and fallen hard for a mysterious man (also, like me); and even like Serena in *Gossip Girl* in the early seasons with Dan.

'I know we're too young to talk about forever, but that's what it feels like,' Serena tells her mum. I think I said pretty much the same thing to mine.

Now I do wonder if how Ezra and I came to be is what set me up for a pattern I would follow far into the future. Without really recognising it, I had learned that we should fight for love, that the best kind of love isn't easy. That you must be patient, and that if you are, it will be better than you had hoped for. And so, emotionally unavailable men would become my kryptonite.

Of course Allie, Bella and Serena had all already taught me this. They got the man eventually, but each had to overcome obstacles and drama to get there. For some of them, it would take years. Essentially, if the journey to becoming someone's girlfriend didn't hurt, you didn't care enough. I thought these women symbolised the gold standard when it came to finding love, and I aspired to experience the same depth of emotion: I didn't yet understand the parts of their relationships that were toxic.

Most of the time Ezra and I spent together was spent at school: I never missed an opportunity to sit on his lap in the common room, and he never missed an opportunity for a rather raunchy French kiss in the hallways. We were not afraid of PDA. I think we thought the more people who saw our tongues entangled, the more obvious it would be how disgustingly in love we were.

He became my confidant too, and for all the malaise I was going through in the classroom, at home, with friends, he would listen and assure me it would be okay. Even if I was the one clearly in the wrong, he would always have my back and assure me I had done the right thing. It was comforting, if not always healthy.

I can still picture us dancing in the street in Bath, drunk on our own love; an afternoon we spent making pizza from scratch, leaving the dough to rise for hours in the airing cupboard while we cuddled on the sofa; the trips into Swindon's dull town centre, made all the more interesting with him by my side.

Six months in, he joined me on a summer trip to California with my sister to meet my dad. The holiday had been booked before we were an item, and three other friends were coming with us too. But still, I was nervous. I wanted my dad to like him; I wanted him to like my dad. Ezra had never been to America, and I needed him to embrace it. It was such a huge part of me. It still is, of course.

As we drove over the Bay Bridge from the airport, Ezra said: 'It looks different. I'm glad, I wanted it to be.'

I looked at him. 'What do you mean?'

'Everything is bigger.' He smiled.

My dad got to know him over the following two weeks, mainly through the medium of teasing him for being a vegetarian. He made a number of dad jokes and Ezra obliged by politely laughing.

One thing I couldn't understand was why my dad wouldn't let us sleep in the same room, even though he knew that my mum had allowed us to in England.

'But, Dad, we sleep in the same bed all the time back home,' I pleaded.

'Fine. But not in my house you don't,' was his response.

And then out of nowhere he made an exception when we stayed two nights in a cosy but slightly creepy cabin on the edges of Lake Tahoe. After we arrived, he simply allocated the rooms, announcing, 'Lizzie and Ezra in the room upstairs; everyone else downstairs.'

My eyes bulged. 'What? But I thought . . .'

'Well this isn't my house, is it?' My dad laughed. It didn't make any sense but I didn't argue.

Time passed quickly as my dad ferried the six of us around in a minivan from San Francisco to Santa Cruz, and many other places in between. All in all, it went better than I could have expected and with my dad's seal of approval, I was even happier.

There's a particular song from that holiday we listened to on repeat on the various road trips, and even now when I hear the first notes, I'm instantly transported back to that minivan and all seven of us singing along, bopping our heads. It's an incredibly happy memory, but it's not a happy song. Rather, it's an Eminem hip-hop number about an abusive relationship, the one he made with Rihanna. I'm not sure either of them imagined it playing in a minivan as the backdrop to two teens falling for each other when they first wrote it.

It's more than a decade later, and I've forgotten Ezra's birthday. Anniversary dates pass me by without recognition, and places that I thought I could never visit again without him have been washed clean of their former meaning. But that song will always remind me of him, of nestling my head into his shoulder as we trundled through the dark. The lyrics still fall out of my lips no matter where I hear it, even though it only happens occasionally now: the gym changing room, a quiet café, the work elevator. The irony being that the words didn't reflect our relationship at all. We felt blissfully happy and madly in love during that time, in a way that only teenagers who haven't been hurt before can be.

For my eighteenth birthday, six months later, Ezra joined my mum, stepdad and sister for dinner at a tapas restaurant. He arrived forty-five minutes late. It was something to do with a university open day and the traffic being terrible and his mum doing something or other. It was completely out of his control, but I was furious. We went outside to argue and I yelled that he didn't put me first. I was hysterical. Later, after I had calmed down and the food had arrived, he put my present on the table. He didn't hand it to me, he just sort of left it there for everyone to examine. It was a small box, wrapped carefully. It looked exactly the same size and shape as a ring box. My heart stopped. My mum and my sister exchanged a glance of concern.

'Happy Birthday,' said Ezra, with a shrug of his shoulders.

I picked it up and twirled it round slowly in my hands. I wanted to open it and I didn't. I hadn't thought at all about the possibility of him proposing, but suddenly there was a microscopic chance that he was about to. And if that was what this box signified, then I would have ruined it all. Both by being unnecessarily horrible for his lateness that night, and for not knowing what to say, even though I loved him. We were so young.

I peeled off the paper and felt the familiar velvet of the ring box before I saw it. I popped it open to reveal a beautiful silver ring with a perfectly pink amethyst at its centre, paired with a row of small diamonds.

I looked at him. My mum looked at him. My sister looked at him. My stepdad looked at him.

'It's not an engagement ring,' he blurted. He had only registered in that moment what we were all thinking; I can't believe he hadn't thought of that before. 'It's just a birthday present. I designed it, my cousin made it,' he continued quickly and bashfully.

'Thank you, it's beautiful.' I kissed him. I could sense the relief around the table. Years later, my mum would tell me she had worried we would get carried away and get married at nineteen; in that moment, it felt like her fear was coming to life.

I wore the ring every day. I was smitten with the way it glinted on my finger, and every time I saw it, I would think of Ezra. News of the ring had spread like wildfire at school, especially because of how much it had cost – a staggering amount for a teenager. Ezra had told one friend, and soon everyone (except me) knew. My mum knew too, as he'd given her the receipt to add to the home insurance. She thought it was far too much. I didn't want to know how much he had spent, but I liked the fact everyone else could tell how serious he felt about me. Or even how crazy he felt about me.

There was one milestone we hadn't marked together yet, and that was sex. I wasn't ready for it and he was patient with me. Everyone at school assumed that we had; only we knew for sure that we hadn't. It became a strange sort of secret between us.

Even my mum assumed we had slept together. One Christmas, she gifted me a see-through nightie with velvet polka dots in front of the entire family. My stepbrother, his then-girlfriend, my stepsister and her then-boyfriend, my sister, Ezra and my stepdad were all there. I could see as I pulled off the wrapping paper what it was, and quickly tucked it back in and said thank you. But my mum wouldn't let the moment pass.

'Oh, what did you get? Why don't you show everyone?'

'Oh it's just some pyjamas, Mum, thanks.'

'Go on, show everyone,' she goaded me.

I held it up for a millisecond, aware I was turning as red as the ornaments on the tree.

My stepsiblings, both a few years older than me, tried to turn a blind eye, but I could see they were holding back laughter. There was a flash between them, too – *What sort of family have we joined?* My sister, more familiar with my mum's tricks, didn't bother hiding her smile. She was just glad it wasn't her in the spotlight.

'Ezra, what do you think?' my mum asked. He looked at me for what to say. In the pause, my mum spoke again: 'Imagine what she'll look like when she's wearing it . . . Imagine what she'll look like when she's *not* wearing it!' She cackled.

'Mum, please, STOP,' I squealed. Ezra shifted uncomfortably in his chair. He was conscious that no response was the right response here, so he chose not to say anything. A wise move.

I'm not religious but my grandmother is, and I had lived with her for a time when I was younger, so her words had always stuck with me when it came to sex: 'Wait until you are married.' She meant so much to me and I didn't want to disappoint her. Okay, I wasn't going to save it for my wedding night, but I was going to take my time until I felt completely ready. And even then, I didn't want it to just happen one Tuesday afternoon when we found ourselves alone in the house. That was too ordinary. Ideally, I wanted a set-up like in *Gossip Girl*, when Serena and Dan fall asleep on Christmas Eve on a mattress in a gallery surrounded by a simulation of falling snow. Could there have been anything more romantic?

But most of all, what I wanted was to avoid being interrupted by our parents. I suggested we find a hotel. Quite bold, based on the fact we were teens who relied on pocket money and payment for the occasional odd job. It meant we had to wait until the right occasion arose.

That's not to say that we hadn't done anything else – we were intimate with each other often – but the actual act felt like a huge leap to me at the time. An irreversible step.

All this meant that we were together for more than a year before we finally had sex. It was a long time, but it felt right to me and I don't regret it – even if it ended up being far from magical. In the end, there was too much pressure, I found it uncomfortable, it wasn't easy – and, for some reason, after all that pent-up waiting and planning, he answered his phone right in the middle of our very first time to none other than his mother. Seriously.

Our bodies were close, his eyes on mine, when I became aware of something vibrating. Had he brought a sex toy with him for our first time? A vibrator? A cock ring? I wasn't sure if I was advanced enough for that. But no, when I looked around the room, I saw his Samsung Galaxy Ace illuminated with the word 'Mum'. Without hesitation, he picked it up.

'Hi Mum . . . Okay, yeah, see you. Yeah, yeah. Okay . . . Bye.'

I would pay serious money to see what my face looked like at that moment. He continued as if nothing had happened.

'What. The Fuck. Are you doing?'

He had completely defeated the point of us being in a hotel where we wouldn't be disturbed.

'I thought if I didn't pick up, she might assume we were having sex or something.' He shrugged.

This was not the magic moment I had been saving myself for by any stretch of the imagination.

'Yeah, well, I still think that would have been better.' I could hardly get the words out, not because I was angry, but because I was laughing. 'She could have waited five minutes,' I deadpanned.

It proved to me that you can plan and plan (our plan included buying a Primark towel to lay down on the hotel bed in case I bled; why I thought this was necessary, I'm not quite sure), but you can't control what happens. Especially when it comes to sex. And on the whole, I was happy; we were happy. It had happened on a weekend away where we felt like adults. That said, I am delighted to say I've never again experienced someone answering the phone to their mother during an intimate moment.

Writing this chapter, I dug deep into my old Facebook messages and found our conversations from when we were dating. I don't recognise the girl in the messages, because she is a girl. Not the woman I continue to become.

They are sickly sweet, filled with kisses and poems, bizarre terms of endearment and declarations of love. In one, Ezra talks about the moment he finally realised he loved me, reiterating the message that our love had been a battle, an uneasy road. I had persisted with him for so long before we got together because I didn't know any better. I thought that was what I had to do, that it would be worth it. And here he was, telling me that it had been.

Now I actively avoid the chase in dating – though it did take me quite a few years to learn that. If someone isn't excited about me from the beginning, then I don't pursue them. I don't want a love interest whom I have to convince; I don't even want someone who feels lukewarm about me. It's the same the other way round, too; I want to be excited for the promise of the next date and eager to tell my friends what it is I like about the person and how they make me feel. I'm not saying there has to be intrigue and passion at every turn, but I want us to be choosing each other and not chasing each other.

With Ezra, there were arguments I had chosen to forget, too. Mainly about trust, about insecurities. The same issues would rear their heads from time to time. Rereading some of his messages is difficult for me now. They make me sad. There are others where I can see Ezra revert to the person he had been before we got together. That makes me sad for him.

Of course, this is from my perspective. I'm sure if Ezra was writing about me, he would say I could be bossy. That I was controlling. That I was jealous. I probably was all those things; we were young and it was my first relationship, one where we both did things and said things we would question now.

Our final holiday together was a cheap package option to Gran Canaria, the summer before university. A nondescript hotel room with two single beds pushed together, a small pool with towels aggressively claiming sunbeds from dawn, and guests walking out of the breakfast buffet with pockets full of bread rolls and cheese (guilty as charged).

We explored the island's giant dunes, went to a nude beach, and ate pizza while looking out at the sea. Yet part of me knew it was the beginning of the end. We'd said that we would stay together; we'd even considered going to the same university to make that easier. But I'd started to feel that might not be the right choice. Partly because I didn't feel ready for such a serious commitment at such a young age – I didn't want to be the girl whose first boyfriend became her husband. It's a beautiful thing to feel sure enough about your first love to know you only want a future where you are together, but that level of devotion didn't feel right for me. I also felt like we might hold each other back. If we chose the same university just to stay together, we would grow resentful. And if we lived far apart and put our relationship first, we'd miss out on the full university experience. Our weekends would be taken up by each other, so there wouldn't be room for as many hobbies or new friends.

I returned to California to spend time with my dad, and I spent more than a month apart from Ezra. With each day, my doubts grew. I didn't miss him the same way I had before, and when his name popped up on my phone, it felt like a chore to reply. I had bought a postcard for him at the beginning of the trip when my dad, sister and I had visited New York, thinking I'd write how one day I hoped we would visit together. But for some reason I'd held off sending it, and I realised that I wasn't sure if that was true anymore.

I never sent the postcard. I didn't know what words to fill it with. They all felt empty.

It was a horrible feeling, falling out of love with Ezra. Slowly but surely, it was as if my skin was peeling off to reveal a new me. I could sense it happening, but I couldn't really explain why or know when the full transformation would be complete. And I couldn't stop it, even if I had wanted to.

What's worse is that I didn't voice how I felt. I just became distant and left him feeling out of sorts and unsure of how the ground had shifted beneath him. He'd end our calls by saying, 'I love you.' It felt like a test, but only because he didn't know how hard it was for me to say it back. Instead, I'd end the call with, 'Lots of love, bye.' It was a subtle difference with an obvious message: I still loved him, but I wasn't in love with him.

It wasn't until the topic of our anniversary came up, though, that I think Ezra properly clocked something had changed over the summer. He kept asking what I wanted to do to celebrate – it was the day after I was due to fly back and he wanted to plan something special. Again and again, I ignored the question. I didn't want him to organise an extravagant day out when I couldn't picture a future for us. Or worse, for him to gift me a handmade present representing soppy memories of us. He had done this before and I had adored it, but it would have been excruciating this time round.

Results day was a mix of emotions, especially as I was still 5,000 miles away: I was ecstatic that both Ezra and I would be heading to our first choice universities. But beneath that there was something gnawing away at me, because it also confirmed that the future we were trundling towards would crash our relationship into a million pieces in a number of weeks. Our new homes would be more than five hours apart and involve a series of convoluted train journeys.

I flew back with my sister, and felt my stomach somersaulting on the ten-hour flight because I knew I couldn't hide how I felt any longer. Once I'd touched down in England, it would be a thudding crash back to earth. I was going to have to face reality – and Ezra.

On the day of our anniversary, he messaged:

> Elizabeth, I'm picking up the vibe that something is pretty wrong. Do you want to say anything now or talk about this face to face? Because I don't really know what to do or what you're thinking – but it's pretty obvious something's changed.

I drove over to his house, and in the car we cried together. I told him I wasn't ready for it to be over, but there was something in my gut that told me it was the only option. He understood, and by this point he had been expecting it.

'I just wish you had said something,' he told me. 'It was horrible not knowing where we stood. I thought maybe you had met someone else.'

It was true that I had fancied other people over the summer; that was part of what had confirmed to me I didn't want to be in a relationship any longer. I'd chat to someone in a café and realise I had butterflies in my stomach. I'd have dinner with family friends and wonder about their son I'd grown up with. There was even a guy I went to school with before I moved to England whom I'd reconnected with, and we'd gone for long hikes in the hills of our hometown. But nothing happened.

The summer apart had been a test without me realising it. Six weeks in different cities would become the norm if we continued, and I wanted to commit fully to a new life in a new place with new friends, and give myself a chance to grow on my own. I also couldn't avoid the fact that Ezra was my first boyfriend, and the only person I had ever kissed. How could I know if this was what I wanted forever?

'There's no one else. I'm sorry. I fucked up. I just didn't want to hurt you.' I shrugged. I knew it was a pathetic excuse, but I was young, had no experience in breaking up and my words were mostly true – there was no point in telling him I had fancied other people, and it wasn't like I was about to start something with anyone from California.

We then made a strange choice. I can't remember who suggested it, but we decided that we would spend the last two weeks we had in Swindon together. Not together like friends, but together as a couple. We didn't want our last memory of each other to be a painful break-up, when for so long we had been happy. Instead, we wanted to honour the relationship that had meant so much to us. But on the day we left for university, that would be it. We'd start university as single people.

And at first, it worked. Knowing there was limited time left together somehow brought us closer than ever before. Plus it meant that, once again, we had a secret. Friends assumed we would stay together, and mention it in passing conversation at the pub. Our eyes would meet, and we'd smile at each other. I had instigated the break-up, but deep down we both knew we needed to try a world where we were apart.

When it came to saying goodbye to our relationship, though, I realised that we'd chosen an incredibly messy and confusing way to break up. At the time, we were convinced that it was the right thing to do, but now I am certain that it was misguided.

The last two weeks we spent together weren't really real; they had been a simulation of our past. It had only been so easy to fall back into a rhythm because we knew it wasn't forever. Our relationship was tied up in school and living at home and the small circle of friends we shared; it didn't include any notion of a future where we would grow up and apart. I knew there was a reason why I had pulled away, but in the weeks and months that followed, it became harder to remember why we'd broken up, because we'd wrapped everything up so neatly. It was unrealistic to think we could build this carefully curated happy memory of us, and then both be able to cut the cord at a pre-prescribed moment in time with no emotions, no sadness.

It also left the door ajar for a rekindling, something I know I have allowed too many times in my love life. Partly it's because I'm a people-pleaser and don't ever want someone to dislike me. Partly it's because I'm a romantic and think that sometimes it's just not the right time, but that doesn't mean it won't ever be. (Spoiler alert: the rekindling inevitably did happen a few years later.)

When I look back now on falling in and out of love with Ezra, it is with bittersweet nostalgia. On the whole, I feel lucky that my first relationship was with him. Mostly, we were kind to each other. Mostly, we cared deeply for each other. Yes, there were things I took away from it that took me a while to unlearn, but I was stronger when I did finally understand those lessons. I knew what I wanted, but also what I didn't want.

And yes, like I said earlier, sometimes I wish I could replicate those fiery feelings of teenage lust and love with someone new. But I also know now that the best kinds of love don't require a roller coaster. You can feel powerful peaks of emotion at any age, and with the right person, you feel them without the troughs. As we age and evolve, we will change our definition of romantic love to fit exactly who we are in that moment and what makes us feel the most content.

Plus, quite frankly, it would be impossible to function if we consistently felt the same intensity of emotion throughout our adult lives. I honestly can't think of anything worse. This isn't a ninety-three-minute movie (the perfect length, in my opinion).

Actually, come to think of it, a Facebook post revealing my pet name with a million xs for all the world to see would be the exact opposite of sexy to me now. But a new flame cleaning my bathroom floor? Hot damn, excuse me while I go lie down.

Some things I've learned about breaking up with someone

- ♥ There's no nice way to do it, but there are certainly nicer ways to do it.

- ♥ Don't even think about ending it over text.

- ♥ Follow the lead of Julia Roberts in *Eat Pray Love*. A decision to leave should always be followed by pizza and pasta (preferably in Italy).

- ♥ Just because you chose to end it doesn't mean you'll be any less heartbroken.

- ♥ You probably shouldn't cry.

- ♥ Dress to feel good, because you won't feel good after.

- ♥ If it's a long-distance relationship, don't wait till the end of the weekend you're spending together, or you'll just look like a liar and a moron.

♥ If you share an apartment, get out fast. You don't want your inner Jennifer Aniston prankster from *The Break-Up* to come out.

♥ For god's sake, tell them as soon as you know. Don't draw it out, don't disappear and don't dissolve on them.

5

TWO DATES AND A GHOSTING

Starring the one who ghosted me

When Ollie disappeared off the face of the planet with no explanation, I fantasised about what I would say to him if I had the chance. Maybe no words were needed. Maybe I'd see him across the room at a bar and embrace my inner romcom heroine by throwing an expensive drink in his face – ideally, with as much class as Samantha Jones in *Sex and the City*, when she shows up in a superb gold dress to meet her cheating ex: 'Dirty martini, dirty bastard.'

Let me get this straight before I delve into the details. I was not sad that Ollie had ghosted me. My reaction to his absence did not involve streams of tears. I have cried over my fair share of boys – I'm not afraid to admit that – but Ollie was not one of them. I was simply flabbergasted by his rudeness.

We'd met on an app, and within a few weeks he'd asked me on a date. Once we'd settled on a time, he sent me a message that read:

> Ok great, you're in the books for next Wednesday! I'm pretty relaxed where, how are your mini golf skills? We could go to puttshack in bank.'

Now, as a small child, I never imagined how integral mini golf would be to my twenty-something dating life. Nor did I predict that during the heyday of these trendy spots opening one a minute in London, it would be near impossible to swing a club without falling into bed with someone. If there was a Venn diagram showing people I have played mini golf with and people I have slept with, it would very nearly be a circle.

The reason for this near-perfect circle being that mini golf is the 'ideal' third date. You've gone for drinks, you've got to know each other, the attraction is definitely there. Maybe you've even branched out to dinner on the second date, the conversation was flowing and you're both intrigued. Now it's time for an activity. Something that suggests you can let loose and have a bit of fun, that you can plan an evening that isn't just dinner or drinks. Though you only have to attend one mini-golf venue on a Thursday post-work to realise the place is filled with nothing but early-stage dates. Choosing mini golf really is as far from showing any sense of individuality as you could hope for. It's beige-flag central. I suppose Ollie marginally broke the mould by suggesting we tee off at our first meeting rather than waiting for the third. From his profile, I could see he was tall, outgoing and into sports – particularly tennis. He had a smattering of freckles and tousled brunette hair. He was hot. I replied:

> My mini golf skills are hit and miss. Sometimes terrible, sometimes not. So up for giving it a go! As long as you're not a total pro.

We met at 6.30pm and grabbed a drink before starting the game. He looked as good as he had in his pictures, with a friendly, expressive face, and we bonded over the fact we'd both lived abroad.

The evening continued much as you'd expect when two people like each other: it was fun, light-hearted and playful. He won by a considerable amount and lapped up the opportunity to tease me about my poor performance. We made up stories about the other couples around us, taking huge leaps from the tiniest of interactions: 'Those two are definitely arch-nemesis colleagues that kissed at the Christmas party.' 'Absolutely. And over there? They met in a spin class and decided they wanted to see each other sweaty again.'

We went back to the seating area, and before long there was a kiss. It was a relief, given that I'd been on a run of hideously dry dates. You know, the ones where you nod your head and smile, all the while wondering when it would be polite to leave, knowing you'd rather be reading a book in bed on your own. That was not the case with Ollie – phew.

Things escalated quickly. He returned from the bar with several shots of tequila, and we returned to a joke from an earlier conversation that we'd go on a weekend break for our second date.

'I've recently decided to be a person that just says why not. How about San Sebastian?' Ollie asked. Before I knew it, he had brought up Skyscanner on his phone. 'There's some decent deals there later in the month.' He grinned.

'I mean, I'm game,' I replied.

I now know that this is one of my downfalls. I take things at face value, and when a man I like says they want to do something or go somewhere, even if it's a bit over the top for a second date, I assume it to be true. Especially if it's more than a flippant comment, and they suggest dates and look up prices. I take it to mean they see a future with me, and I get excited about what our new fling could one day be. Partly because I'm spontaneous and I want my future partner to be spontaneous too; partly because I want a romcom-style love story – and I'm sure I'm not alone in that.

How many couples do you know who say they met in a pub or through friends, only to later fess up that they met on Tinder? It's because it feels clinical and boring, too contrived. And so if I was going to meet someone on an app, I loved the idea that part of our story also included a second date where we sipped sangria on a beach in Spain. I wanted excitement, intrigue. To be so caught up in the heady first days of mutual attraction that we behaved in a way we could not explain. I know now that isn't always the recipe for lasting love, and that finding excitement in the simplest of dates can mean so much more.

Plus, more often than not, these grand ideas are just empty flirting. They rarely turn into reality. Frankly, anyone who mentions making big future plans before you've even said your first goodbye is quite unlikely to stick around, at least in my experience. The same goes for anyone who engages in any kind of love-bombing. Simply put: Ollie had no intention of booking a flight to the Spanish coast with me, that month or ever. Indeed, the fact he'd suggested this with no immediate action was my first red flag. But I didn't know that yet.

We arranged another date a week or so later. Ollie suggested a Monday. Red flag. I told him he could be in charge of organising what to do, seeing as he chose such a rogue day. He said he would, and then the day before asked me if I had any go-to bars. I ended up choosing the spot. Red flag. A few hours before we had planned to meet, he explained that he was slammed at work and asked if we could raincheck to the following week. Red flag. Come to think of it, it was a hat-trick of red flags.

Okay, so at this point, things weren't looking quite as promising. I certainly got the sense that I wouldn't be pulling out my passport with him anytime soon. But he did ask if there was a charge at the bar for cancelling at the last minute, and he did apologise multiple times, so I decided to let it slide.

The following Monday rolled around, and there were no hiccups this time. We met to drink wine in an underground bar, and the chat was just as fun and flirty as it was before. He pulled up a note on his phone of bars and restaurants he wanted to try in London, and suggested we choose one for the next date. I liked his confidence. He told me about a holiday to the Philippines;

I filled him in on my birthday night out. We spoke about our younger sisters: how they both live in different countries, how much we miss them, how close we are to them. The only red flag that night was the fact he admitted he didn't like cheese. Not even mozzarella. What a weirdo.

We ended up going home together and sleeping together. It was easy and nice. I felt comfortable in his presence. I thought that I would like to see him again. When he left, he said, 'See you soon. I'll text you.' I believed him.

A couple of days went by and I heard nothing. I wasn't waiting for a text or overthinking, because I just assumed I would hear from him. He'd said that he would text me. I found it strange but not concerning. I sent him a short message asking how his week had been. He didn't reply.

That weekend, I went to visit Rebecca. I posted a series of Instagram stories of our night out, and he watched every single one. Yes, he had asked to follow me on the first date; yes, that should have been another red flag. At this point, I really should have spotted him for who he was: it was giving 'useless second male lead' energy.

But instead I thought it must have been a mistake, or there must have been some reason, so I sent another message a week later. All it said was:

Yoooo?

Not my finest example of great communication, but I just wanted to see if I could prod him into giving some explanation or rejection or anything. No reply.

I was in disbelief at his rudeness. Surely, I thought, if you've slept with someone, you can have the decency to give even the lamest of excuses. Tell me work is intense. Tell me your hay fever is bad. Tell me your dog has died. I wasn't asking for much: a single text would have sufficed.

When I told my younger sister, she just laughed. 'What? You've never been ghosted? That's hilarious.'

Thank you for your words of comfort, Kate. I had been ghosted before, but not by someone I'd slept with.

I also knew that we worked in the same neighbourhood; we'd never bumped into each other before, but it was a real possibility. Had he not considered this? Would it not be so much less awkward if there had already been some acknowledgement? Some closure of sorts? I imagined what I would say to him if our paths crossed. I never thought they actually would, and definitely not any time soon.

But then, exactly that happened. It was two weeks since we'd last seen each other, five days since my unanswered follow-up text. I was walking into work at about 9am, coming from a slightly different direction from normal. I'd just hopped off the bus and there, no more than ten feet in front of me, was Ollie. I did a double-take.

And, unfortunately for Ollie, on that particular morning I was channelling a great big don't-fuck-with-me energy. I was freshly showered, hair blow-dried, and I was ready for a takedown. There was no way I was going to let this moment slip away without saying my piece. How often do you get this chance? Yes, I could have ducked my head and avoided eye contact, but I felt I had a duty to myself, and also to other women. Ollie needed to know he couldn't get away with acting like a twat.

I had a split second to decide how best to approach it – the charm offensive or angry lecture. I marched over with a dangerous smile on my face, thinking the right move was somewhere between the two.

'Hi, Ollie,' I said. I had caught him off-guard; he hadn't seen me coming.

'Oh Lizzie, hi. Sorry, I owe you a text, don't I?' he said. His eyes had flashed with alarm when he first registered who was in front of him, but he had quickly transitioned to calm and collected.

The cad was going to try to make this seem like some misunderstanding on my part. 'Sorry, been really busy.'

I shook my head, still smiling and considering my choice of words. The conversation hadn't escalated yet, but there was a certain energy between us, and I knew I wasn't the only one to feel it, because the other commuters around us were clearly slowing down to try and catch the conversation. Even strangers could somehow sense this wasn't going to be a friendly chit-chat.

I didn't hold back. 'Actually, Ollie, I think what happened is that you slept with me and then you ghosted me.'

'Uh . . .' he began.

But I wasn't finished: 'Yes. We had sex, I texted you, you ignored me. Repeat. Do you feel good about that?'

His eyes widened; he clearly hadn't expected me to be so up front. He clearly didn't know me very well. 'Oh, um, I'm so sorry. It's just . . . Do you have time to get a coffee so I can explain myself?'

I laughed in an irritated way. 'No I don't have time to get a coffee. I'm on my way to work – and I don't want to.' I shook my head in disbelief. 'I can't believe you're trying to play this down like you're some nice guy.'

I remembered him telling me on our second date how lucky he felt he was to have a sister, because it had taught him to be a more respectful man, especially when it came to dating. I wasn't planning on bringing it up at this moment, but this particular detail had wriggled under my skin and I could still feel it there, gnawing away. That he had used his sister to make him seem more thoughtful and understanding when he had so little decency. Was this how he would want his sister to be treated?

The words were falling out of my mouth before I had time to process them or think of something more witty. 'Oh, and one more thing, that thing you said about how having a sister has made you more respectful? What. A load. Of shit.' I wish I had been more eloquent, but I didn't have a team of scriptwriters behind me to workshop that specific moment: this was just a chance encounter that I wasn't going to get again.

'I know; I really am sorry. I don't normally do this. And I do really want to explain myself. Let's go for a coffee next week. Please?' He took a step towards me.

'Fine. Maybe – I don't know. I've got to go.' I walked past him, the exhilaration of the moment pulling me forward. I felt incredible. I hadn't had an expensive drink in my hand to throw in his face, but that was probably a good thing. The important bit was that I'd had my chance to say my piece. I felt just as empowered as Samantha Jones.

And Samantha isn't the only one. There's always that pivotal scene in a romcom where the heroine sacks off her loser boyfriend or the date that has treated her poorly; a moment that shows us that our main character values herself more than the pursuit of romantic love. I love these moments because they are often silly and entertaining and outrageous. It's never just a quietly sad conversation in a generic coffee shop with a bad playlist in the background; there's two punches and a knee to the groin at prom or a killer line with a jaw drop and a turn of the heel. And these moments are also empowering. In a genre that is so much about getting the guy, these scenes remind us that some men just aren't worth it.

One of my favourites is in *A Cinderella Story*, when Hilary Duff's character tells her romantic interest: 'Waiting for you is like waiting for rain in this drought. Useless and disappointing.' Her cutting words are so powerful, and it was an important message to me as a teen, that one of the best things you can do is stand up for yourself. In this case, they do end up together, but only because she stopped letting him treat her badly.

Before I'd even reached the office, my phone vibrated.

> Hey Lizzie, morning. I'm glad I bumped into you earlier, I needed that jolt. Really poor form from me, and I'm really sorry for my behaviour. It was immature and I can do better. Let's grab a coffee next week and chat. Hope work goes ok.

I didn't reply until the evening. I didn't want to at all, but I figured that would have been hypocritical of me. I sent him a cursory message, thanking him for the apology. I hoped that would just shut the conversation down.

He replied straight away:

> Thanks for not slapping me, you were within your rights to.

I took a second look. Was he really turning this into some sort of light-hearted, flirty joke? It seemed a bizarre way to respond. Then again, maybe it made him feel better about the way he had acted and helped ease his conscience that he wasn't in fact a total fuckboy. It was all a joke; he was always going to reply. Except he wasn't.

I wasn't angry anymore, though; those negative feelings I'd been carrying around for days had lifted as soon as I had stepped away from him.

I said I was glad I had bumped into him and sorry if I had been blunt, but I had needed to say something about it. I couldn't let him walk all over me. Now that was done, I had nothing left to say.

He did, though. Indeed, he had plenty to say. For someone who couldn't formulate a one-sentence reply just days earlier, he now suddenly had entire essays to get off his chest. He persisted with his request for a coffee, and even suggested we meet for a drink again in the future. I was beginning to find the whole thing hysterical.

I wondered if the fact I'd been assertive and called him out had turned him on. If the fact I had shown I was no longer interested had suddenly made me more attractive to him. If, after all that, he was trying to get us back on a romantic path once again.

But then I received the following. Which is obviously the opposite of a sexy text. Hold your breath.

> If you want the context before we meet: 1) I spent the past 6 months trying to sell one of my companies that would have given me enough cash – for my 15% stake – to de-risk my life and buy, in cash, a flat in Hampstead. The other company pulled out a day before signing and now my company has less than 2 months of cash left to continue trading before it becomes insolvent. It'll mean losing c.100 jobs and the best part of 5 years of my life going up in smoke. 2) a couple of my other companies are facing huge cashflow problems and we laid off 5 people this week and will need to get rid of the same again over the next couple of weeks. They have mortgages and families, but the company doesn't have the cash in reserve. 3) I found out my ex is dating another of the guys at my tennis club, and I'm embarrassed and don't know how to process it.

> That's a big overshare and I should have just sent you a one-line text to say I needed a time-out, but I didn't know what to say. I'm sorry.

I had been on two dates with this man. He was trying to make up for his earlier silence, sure, but I really didn't need to know all this. I said not to worry and that I hoped it would all sort itself out.

Later, when I told several friends about how I'd seen the man who'd ghosted me and chosen to confront him, I felt proud. One friend actually gave me a high-five. On another day, I might have avoided eye contact with him at all costs, but for whatever reason I'd seen it as my moment and I'd taken it. Thank god.

It made me think about ghosting and why it feels so cruel. For me, it comes down to this: it's not just the fact that the other person hasn't deemed you important or worthy enough to take a few seconds out to let you know they're no longer on the same page, it's that they rob you of the opportunity to say how you feel. It diminishes your worth, it makes you feel small, it casts you into the role of the scorned party. It took having my own chance with Ollie to realise all those dramatic movie break-up scenes where the main character takes control are important for another reason. It's because they give that character a voice. I was glad I got to have mine; I didn't want Ollie's ghostly shadow hanging over me.

Ollie and I did exchange a few friendly messages over Instagram from time to time after that, and he did ask me out for a drink nearly a year later. What inspired him to do that, and whether he intended it to be as friends or something more, I don't know, because I didn't go. I had decided that once someone becomes a ghost, you can't bring them back from the dead.

I don't have a single bad feeling towards him anymore, though. I wasn't that invested and I don't think he ever meant to be rude or cruel. He simply got caught up in his own life and took the easy route out. I'd like to think he wouldn't do it again to someone else. At the very least, maybe he'll think of me next time it crosses his mind, and then decide a text really is the easier option.

But who knows? He's not my problem anymore. And in my experience, people who ghost their dates rarely change. I just hope whoever is next holds him to account too. And not for his benefit, but for their own.

Some things I've learned about red flags

♥ Red flags are red for a reason. Don't ignore them.

♥ When they say you are perfect on the first date, alarm bells should start ringing.

♥ If they refer to themselves as an alpha male, get out now.

♥ Don't stick around if you see them being rude to hospitality staff – there's a lot worse coming.

♥ Men who tell you to smile more? Barf.

♥ Stalking is never romantic, no matter what *Sleepless in Seattle* portrays.

♥ The line 'My humour is a little controversial' is code for 'I'm a racist, sexist asshole.'

♥ Scan his bookshelf: there are no excuses for owning a copy of *The Game*.

♥ Men that only talk about themselves on the first date are not going to suddenly become great listeners.

- ♥ Beige flags are also important to look out for: strong opinions on pineapple pizza, claiming their personality is like a golden retriever, any quote relating to *The Office* on their dating profile.

- ♥ If their ex was a 'crazy psychopath', there's a strong chance *they* are actually the crazy psychopath.

- ♥ Nate in *The Devil Wears Prada*? Sorry, he's the biggest red flag of them all.

- ♥ Some red flags are international, but you'll need to study the local specifics for whatever city you're in. Here are some examples:

  - In New York: they live in Murray Hill.

  - In LA: they have an acting headshot on their dating profile.

  - In Paris: they wear a beret unironically.

  - In Madrid: their favourite Spotify playlist is 'Top 50 España'.

  - In Melbourne: they invite you on a coffee date and then order a hot chocolate.

- ♥ Sometimes you have to go through a season (read: multiple years) of running towards red flags in order to learn how to run in the opposite direction.

6

THE HOSTEL DIARIES

Starring the one who helped me get over an ex

My favourite way of getting over someone? Booking a spontaneous trip somewhere fun. Preferably without a return ticket. This isn't always possible, but if you can make it work, even if it's just a day trip to a nearby seaside town, trust me – it can work wonders.

In this case, though, my trip was to Nice in the south of France, during a long summer at university. I'd even convinced someone via email to give me a job in a hostel so I'd have a place to live rent-free and some spending money.

The reason for this much-needed escape stemmed from the fact that I'd made the mistake of giving my first love, Ezra (MSN boy), a second chance a couple of years after we broke up. We had started messaging each other again and I knew we were both single; then, at a New Year's party back home, the flirting went up a notch. I realised I had forgotten my keys, so he kindly offered up his brother's empty bed. I know, I know. I saw his ulterior motive coming a mile off and I didn't care at all. I lapped it up. My mum texted later to say she'd left the door on the latch. I conveniently forgot to tell him. I can be sneaky too.

Not long after midnight, we were walking through the streets of the town we went to school in, laughing and touching each other in a way that could have been just friendly – or could have easily been something more. We were nervous, testing the waters. A playful shove, a gentle hand on a cheek for a fleeting moment. When we stumbled through his porch door, like we had done so many times before, it suddenly felt all too familiar. Like we had gone back in time.

I hadn't had anything as serious as what we'd once had in the time we'd been apart, and I had started to wonder if we really were meant to be together, but we'd just met too young. Had our youth clouded my judgement? I'd broken up with him to see what else was out there, but I hadn't exactly gone wild at university. I'd kissed a few boys, I'd fancied one or two more than the others, but I had not fallen in love and I had not had sex with anyone else. I'd even been jealous when he'd had another girlfriend, and thought that maybe I'd missed my chance.

I know now that these emotions were rooted in first-love illusion. My memory of our relationship was so tied up with nostalgia that I was chasing the feelings we'd had together rather than a person.

'Do you want a glass of water?' he asked.

'Yes, please.'

He filled two glasses from the tap. I stood on the other side of the kitchen, taking in the space that had once been so everyday to me. We climbed the stairs and he showed me into his brother's room, even though I knew where it was. We said goodnight, he loitered for a moment longer than necessary and then closed the door.

It was freezing, so I swiftly crawled under the covers, but I couldn't help wondering what it would mean if something happened. I debated whether I should have made some sort of move. I knew that I still could, as he was just across the hallway. But before I could decide what to do, the door creaked open and he stepped into the room: 'Hi.'

'Hi,' I replied.

It wasn't a one-off, either. He visited me for my birthday and I made the trek to see him in return. There had been something supremely comforting about slipping into old patterns, reverting to our favourite pet names and in-jokes, recounting shared memories and holding each other once again.

It didn't last. Things ended, and then on a totally normal boring afternoon, some time later, I opened Facebook to find a photo that made my heart collapse into a million pieces. It was a picture of Ezra with his arm around the woman I had been jealous of before. My jealousy hadn't stopped when they broke up, either. And so while it was a bombshell, I had half-expected it. The caption is still seared into my mind. It was soppy and sweet and it made me desperately sad.

Yes, I had been the one to end our first relationship, but on the second go-round it was me that was struggling to get over the fact we had ended once again. I knew it hadn't been quite the same as what we'd had before, but it was reassuring in a way I hadn't expected. It felt safe.

Finding out that he'd moved on so quickly, though, really set me off. I cried a lot, in particular to my housemates Annie, Jess and Alice. I felt like a fool.

On the night I saw the picture, Ezra and I had a phone call that went on for hours.

Annie messaged me despite being in the same house:

> I am getting into PJs and reading my book, but I won't be going to sleep for a while. I'll leave my door ajar so just knock and come in, even if my light's off x

That is the kind of friendship I look for – and that is the kind of friendship I want to offer.

This is actually one of the upsides of heartbreak: seeing what your crew will do to help you through it. It might be travelling from one end of the Northern line to the other just to sit on your bed with smoothies and sweets, or it might be sending you a plant in the post. (Alice did this one time, a potted peace lily that I decided to name after the ex in jest. All I can say is thank god she didn't keep up this tradition for every break-up, or I might be living in a conservatory to rival Kew Gardens by now. I could charge £20 for entry and call it Botany of a Broken Heart.)

But even with my friends rallied around me, I quickly realised I didn't want to spend the summer in Swindon knowing Ezra would be there too. Yes, I was moving to Paris as part of my degree in the autumn, but that was still ten weeks away. Going home and knowing he'd be at the pub whenever our friends got together wasn't going to help me get over him.

And then I found the aforementioned job in a hostel in the south of France and booked a flight. I was channelling my inner Colin Firth's Jamie in *Love Actually*, matching the way he escaped to France after catching his girlfriend sleeping with his brother. I guess at least I was grateful I didn't have to deal with the whole sibling betrayal – thanks, Kate. (You'd be surprised by how many times men joke about fancying your siblings or your mum; though, if you're a straight woman, maybe you wouldn't.) In the film, Jamie had already planned his trip and originally the girlfriend was meant to accompany him, but he ended up going solo instead. And the time away allowed him to forget and open his heart again. I hoped it would do the same for me.

The night before I was due to fly off on my French Riviera adventure, I didn't go to bed until long after midnight. I've never been one to pack in advance, which was part of the reason I was still awake, but I was also so bloody nervous. It hadn't hit until then that while a solo summer in Europe was the stuff that Lizzie McGuire's dreams are made of, it was also extremely intimidating. Was it really wise to be leaving my friends behind while I was going through heartbreak? Was I pushing myself to do something I wasn't ready for?

I landed in the morning to find Nice positively sweltering. The first bad sign was that I couldn't find the hostel. Perhaps I was delirious from the heat, or more likely I wasn't that good at map reading – this was before I had a smartphone – but I must have looped the cobbled streets of the old town with a bag bigger than me for a good thirty minutes before I finally found the door to the hostel. It turned out I had walked past it three times already thanks to the fact there was no sign, just a name on the buzzer.

I rang it and, after a pause, someone answered. '*Bonjour?*'

'Hello, I mean, *bonjour. Je suis la nouvelle réceptionniste?*'

'What? Are you here for the hostel?'

'Yes, I am, I'm here for the job? The receptionist?'

'Um, sorry I'm not sure . . . I'll buzz you up.'

That was the second bad sign. I stepped into the hallway and began to climb the steps to the entrance on the third floor. I tried not to focus on the fact that the woman on the other end of the buzzer didn't seem to be expecting me. I knew that if I did, I might just end up bursting into tears, what with the heat and the stairs (and the heartbreak). I reasoned with myself: I'd organised the work with a man, the owner. Maybe he'd just forgotten to tell the rest of the staff.

I pushed on the door and emerged into a small reception, with huge backpacks piled up in one corner, a couple of computers in the other, and a small desk with a very blonde woman behind it. There were a few other travellers slumped around, charging their phones.

I walked over to the blonde woman and tried, in broken French, to explain again who I was.

She smiled. 'I'm Estonian, actually, so we can speak in English.'

I blushed.

'But the owner isn't here right now, and sorry, he didn't tell me you were coming. We just hired someone to replace me when I leave next week, so I'm a bit confused,' she continued.

The panic was making my throat feel like it was closing up. I was meant to be living in the hostel. I didn't have a back-up plan. Had I just flown to another country without a job or a place to stay? I was supposed to be gallivanting round on the back of some beautiful European man's scarlet moped, completely carefree and ready to perform a pop concert to thousands by now, like in *The Lizzie McGuire Movie*, not having a breakdown.

'Oh, okay. I only organised it a few weeks ago. I spoke with Louis – I think he's the owner? We agreed I would arrive on this date.'

'Look, he should be here in five minutes. Just sit there for a moment and I'm sure he'll clear it all up,' she said as she picked up a mop and bucket.

When forty-something Frenchman Louis did arrive, he said he hadn't been sure if I would turn up – he never did explain why, given that we had confirmed it via email – but not to worry, it would all be fine.

'Why don't you leave your stuff, go explore and come back in two hours? I'll have figured out a bed for you by then and you can start work tomorrow.' He grinned.

'Leave my stuff here?' I asked.

'Yes – you don't want to just sit around waiting, do you?' He chuckled.

'Uh, no, no, I guess not. Okay, I'll come back . . . at three?'

'See you.' He was already turning around to attend to something else.

Moments later I was back on the streets of the old town, still sweating and even more frazzled than I had been when I had first arrived. My mind jumped from thought to thought: *Maybe these bad signs are telling me to get the hell out of here? Maybe I'm a fucking idiot for thinking I could do this on my own and should book a return flight home pronto? Maybe I should get an ice cream?*

I decided on the latter. It was the easiest decision: pistachio. I could answer the other questions later. And so I ambled around, perusing a nearby antiques market, watching the rollerbladers along the promenade, and eyeing up the various boats in the port. I even ended up bumping into a friend of a friend on the main shopping street: she was working in Nice for the summer too, and for none other than my new boss's girlfriend. It was comforting to know how small the world can be; it helped me to realise I had to give the summer a shot. I couldn't run from it just because the first day was hard or scary. Indeed, maybe the fact it felt hard and scary was exactly what would make this summer one of my favourites.

When I returned later, I was told the hours I would be working on reception, and shown to a room with a bunk bed and another single bed. I had a job and a place to sleep. The bedroom was shared with the two other receptionists, an Irish girl called Rachel and a Portuguese guy named Gonçalo. The room was small and the door was broken off its hinges, so you had to actually pick it up off the ground and move it to get in and out, but I could see it becoming home. That night, Rachel and I stayed up late in the kitchen chatting. She was at the end of her year abroad, so she had plenty of tips to share. It also turned out that she and Gonçalo weren't exactly about to get ill-advised matching friendship tattoos anytime soon, so my arrival was perfectly timed.

Over the following weeks, Rachel and I spent numerous hours together and became fast friends. It was hard not to bond when we were faced with so many ridiculous situations.

There was the time we had to carry countless heavy and unwieldy beds through the old town from one building to another, dodging clueless tourists and pivoting round tight corners. We were sweating buckets and screaming expletives as we navigated the stairs. There was the time someone reported a bad smell in one of the rooms, and we were sent to find out why. We thought maybe it would just be someone's smelly socks. Instead, we found a plastic bag on top of the cupboard full of nothing other than human shit. I kid you not. We retched and gagged and cried tears of laughter imagining what series of unfortunate events led a guest with no other choice but to do that. There was the time we caught medium-ugly lads on tour with too much confidence pissing off the balcony and had to kick them out. That was rather satisfying.

Not to mention the countless times we offered to show the people hanging round reception the best bars in town in exchange for a few drinks, and ended up dancing on tables at Aussie bar Wayne's. Some guests were nice, some were extremely weird; it didn't matter as long as they had a penchant for buying rounds of shots. We'd return home at an ungodly hour, eat food out of the fridge that didn't belong to us, and then repeat the next day. One time there was even a tub of Ben & Jerry's Cookie Dough, and we felt like we'd hit the jackpot. We left the owners a note inside the empty pot saying, 'Thanks for helping out two very drunk girls.' Good karma would almost definitely come their way.

We knew all the important people (ahem, all the bartenders) and we danced through the streets as if they were our own. The tourists would come and go each week, but we were part of the city's fabric now. Or at least that's how it felt. When another Irish girl, Aoife, joined as a cleaner and Jasmine, who was English like me, as another receptionist, our gal-pal crew was complete. We were the Sisterhood of the French Riviera, the Mean Girls of the Med.

They say you can't run away from your problems, but I couldn't help but feel I had. Once I gave my summer away a chance, I was having too much fun to worry about some boy and his boring summer back home.

Gonçalo kept his distance as predicted; he'd rollerblade through reception with his top off and not bother to say goodbye.

He'd switch off the lights from his top bunk while Rachel and I were mid-conversation with no warning.

Never mind – I had my new girl gang. Together, we'd gossip about all the guests and give them nicknames: the ones we loved, the ones we hated, the ones we thought were strange. There was Kevin Senior, a timid Hungarian man in his late forties with a uniform of football jerseys and sweatpants. He seemed harmless, but also totally out of place. There was the hopeless romantic from Canada, who paid us to deliver a bouquet of flowers so big it took two of us to carry it to a woman he had spent two hours with – and had already decided he would definitely marry. There were the eighteen-year-old Aussie assholes who couldn't handle their drink and left a pile of sick a worrying shade of green in the corner of the room for us to clean up.

And, of course, there were the ones we fancied. For me, it was a beautifully tanned and tall Dutch man who stayed for weeks on end. He paid for his hostel stay with a sack of coins he'd earned busking on the promenade; I didn't mind counting out the small change, as it meant more time together. He also had the most incredible voice, so I forgave him for being that tired hostel cliché of 'man with a guitar'. The difference was he had talent. Or maybe it was that he was a total dreamboat. Or, more likely, a combination of the two. We took the bus to a nearby seaside village and drank two-euro red wine from the bottle while eating Brie with our hands on a picnic blanket on the sandy beach. The sun warmed our skin and we went for dips in the sea. I was besotted. He was unaware.

I told my mum, and three days later she wrote on my Facebook page:

> How's it going with the beautiful Dutch man? Xxx

I didn't notice it for at least an hour, at which point I let out a shrill yelp, deleted it, and then called her to once again explain the difference between a wall post and a private message.

'Oh, I didn't realise everyone could read my private messages to you,' she said, unbothered.

'It's not a message though, Mum, it's a wall post.' I tried not to sound too cantankerous.

I don't think the Dutch man saw the message anyway, and if he did it certainly didn't spring him into action. But there was no shortage of men to fancy and flirt with, and I surprised myself by not thinking of Ezra at all. In Swindon, something as bland as eating a dough ball at Pizza Express could have triggered a hideous meltdown. But in Nice, there was nothing to remind me of him.

In between the countless nights out, Rachel, Aoife, Jasmine and I would go on mini expeditions, sometimes catching the bus to Cannes and Antibes and Eze, or a train across the border to Italy. The hostel owner Louis told us, 'If you want to meet an eligible man, you should go to Monaco.' We went – and promptly disagreed with him. Rich? Certainly. Eligible? Not in our opinion.

We ate our weight in fro-yo and gelato, and went island-hopping and on long hikes and to aqua parks; we rented bikes and dared each other to dive into the water from great heights. We saw people having sex up against a wall in an alleyway with a surprisingly spectacular view, and witnessed a possible Mafia shooting in an outdoor restaurant, all in the same day. We found a late-night bakery that became a favourite place to soak up the alcohol, and ordered pizza after pizza. We laughed at the guests who hadn't realised the shower doors were on back to front, and you had to hang your towel just so if you didn't want people to see you naked. We told each other stories and we laughed and we loved each other.

*

By the end of the summer, our mood on the nights out – which were practically daily – had changed. We were tired of meeting new people who would shortly disappear, and just wanted to be with the motley crew we had formed of all our different friends living there for the season. Those of us who were single were also tired of being hit on by men who would be in the city for one or maybe two nights before moving on – men whose only chat-up line was likely to be, 'Where are you from?' I was blonder than ever before thanks to all the hours in the sun, so when I'd reply that I was from Swindon, the man in question would always ask, 'Sweden?', and I'd simply nod my head. It was easier and it didn't matter – they didn't really care where I was from. The only time this backfired was when the man in question was from Sweden himself, and he quickly realised I could not speak the language. I pretended to be too drunk and ran off before I found out if he thought my lie was funny or rude.

Francesco approached me in exactly this way. I was standing at the bar, having just engaged in a round of blow-job shots – a mix of Bailey's and Amaretto topped with a squirt of crème Chantilly, which we did routinely purely for the ridiculous name – when he tapped me on the shoulder. I wiped the whipped cream from my upper lip.

'Where are you from?' he asked.

'I'm not going to tell you,' I said.

'Why?' He laughed.

I could tell he thought I was being flirty, but I actually wasn't. 'Because I've been asked that exact question a million times in this exact bar this summer,' I replied.

'Oh, do you live here?'

'Yes.' I sighed and went to turn away.

'You don't look French. I grew up here. I live in Paris now.' He wasn't giving up. This did at least snag my interest; he wasn't a tourist, and he lived in the city I was due to move to in a few weeks' time. He had an alluring accent, too.

'Ha ha no, I'm English. Well, half-English, half-American.'

'I'm Italian, but I've always lived in France.'

'And you said you live in Paris now? I've been working at a hostel here, but I'm actually moving there soon.'

'To Paris? Wow. What's your name?'

'It's Lizzie.'

'Your full name, I mean. I'm going to add you on Facebook.'

'What, right now?'

'Yeah.' He brought out his phone and pulled up the app. 'Lizzie . . .'

I hesitated. 'I just met you. You can ask me my full name later.'

'But what if we lose each other and we regret it forever?'

If this line sounds like I made it up, remember that Francesco is European. And not just European, but a deadly, dangerous mix of French and Italian. If British men underplay their emotions, French and Italian men overplay them. They are the kings of romantic lines, of heightened emotions. And I fucking love it.

'Fine. It's Frainier,' I said. And then I left him to go and dance with my friends.

We kept catching each other's eyes the rest of the night, and when the girls and I left later to go to an even dirtier and sweatier club called Pompeii, he was there too. But it was loud, we didn't talk much and I didn't bother to say goodbye.

The next morning, I had a friend request. Francesco De Luca. Annoyingly, his profile was private.

My finger hovered. I hadn't decided if he was worth wasting my time on just yet, but it did cross my mind that a) it would be rude not to accept his proffering of friendship considering he was a local and I was not, and b) I wouldn't be able to decide if I was interested until I'd seen more photos. My memory of him the previous night was already hazy.

I hit 'accept' and then scrolled through. My jaw dropped. He was hot – really fucking hot. Easily over six foot and lean, with short dark chocolate hair and chiselled abs – actual abs! He dressed extremely well and his face was devastatingly handsome. And he was an Italian living in Paris. What the hell had I been thinking?

'Jasmine. Rachel. Why did you let me ignore this perfect, beautiful man?'

Within minutes, he had invited me to a Facebook event: POOLPARTY2K13. I looked over the details. It was an annual party he hosted at his family's home, with pictures from previous years and thirty or so people already attending. There was going to be lots of booze and ping-pong tournaments and an amazing pool with a far-reaching view over the beautiful French countryside. And it was on Saturday night.

Rachel was leaving for her final year at university on Friday, and Aoife had to work.

'Jasmine, what do you think? Should we go to this party? There's no way I'm going on my own. I mean, I think I spoke to the man for a minute max,' I said.

'How often do you get invited to a pool party by a local? I think we should do it,' she said.

'Okay, I'll tell him we're coming and find out how to get there. Eeek.'

The house was in a town perched on a hill inland from Nice. By car, it was just twenty-five minutes. By bus, as we would most certainly be doing it, it was nearly an hour. The last one left at 8pm.

I asked Francesco:

> What about getting back though? is there a night bus?

He replied:

> First one in the morning! like 6am.

Jasmine and I realised we couldn't just go for a couple of hours and decide to bail. If we wanted to be at the party, we had to fully commit to keeping the fun going until 6am. We went back and forth all week. On Saturday, we decided we had to go or we'd regret it, and would spend the rest of our time wondering what it would have been like. This was one of those opportunities that you couldn't just let pass you by. We'd figure out a way home if we really needed to – that was a future problem. Not a now problem. And in that moment, all we knew was that we wanted to go.

We got ready in the hostel and then boarded the bus in the evening. I'd written the instructions on a small piece of paper: the bus stop, the road to take, where to turn right, the number of the house. I actually still have that piece of paper; it's crumpled and dried out, having got sodden from my unexpected entrance to the pool. More on that later.

However, we hadn't banked on it getting dark before we got there, and as the light left the sky, we realised it was impossible to read the bus-stop signs as we whizzed past. When I asked the driver to let us know where to get off, he told us we'd already missed our stop. Luckily, we hadn't gone too far past it. He stopped the bus on a random kerb and gestured for us to get off.

We had no other choice, so we began walking in the opposite direction along a road in what felt like the middle of nowhere in the pitch black. To go to a random guy's house in a town we'd never been to before. We couldn't stop laughing at the situation we found ourselves in.

'What if we can't find the house?' I giggled.

'Oh my god. What will we do? We can't even get home now; we're just going to have to call him and get him to come find us.' Jasmine had to stop walking from the laughter.

But we did find the house, and we knew it was the right one because we could hear music and the chatter of people drifting down from above. Admittedly, it didn't sound as busy or as rowdy as we were expecting. But it was too late to chicken out now. I rang the buzzer and peered through the imposing gate. There was a long driveway leading up, and before long I could see Francesco waltzing down it, waving at us.

'You made it! Welcome.' He buzzed us in and kissed us both on both cheeks. So European. So classy.

We walked up to the party, which wasn't at all what we had expected. His parents were there, as were some of his cousins, and friends too, but it became obvious everyone knew each other and had done since they were children at school. Forget wild summer pool party, we had turned up to a family barbecue. We stuck out like two sore thumbs. We set our bags down in the house and then went outside to join the party.

'So, how do you know Francesco?' one girl asked me and Jasmine.

'Oh, we met him in Wayne's last week.'

The mention of Wayne's was all it took. Her face became pinched and she smiled a knowing smile before walking away. I could have sworn I heard her say something about us to the rest of the group, referring to me and Jasmine only as '*les Anglaises*' – the English girls.

But Francesco was welcoming and kept pouring us drinks, and as the evening went on and everyone became drunker, everyone was a little friendlier. There was a punchy punch, and litres and litres of beer, and more Jägermeister than you would ever want. Admittedly, that's not too hard, as who has ever wanted more than one shot of the stuff? Jasmine and I joined in for the ping-pong tournament and were halfway decent. We didn't embarrass ourselves, at least. Eventually, the family members disappeared, and the atmosphere changed almost instantly.

Francesco grabbed my hand and led me down to the pool. We sat on a sun lounger away from everyone else up at the house and got the chance to properly talk. I realised he was older than I had initially thought, but it didn't bother me. He told me about the small business he owned; his arty hobbies that filled his nights and weekends. Everything he said made me more attracted to him. His life in Paris sounded exciting, and I realised I wanted to be a part of it.

After half an hour or so, he looked up at the stars. 'I love to come and sit here when I'm home to look at the constellations,' he mused.

I shoved him. 'I'm not falling for that pathetic line.'

'Yes you are.' He smiled, and then he leaned in and kissed me. Okay, maybe I was a little bit.

I looked into his ocean-blue eyes and felt a wave pull me under. I knew then I was in trouble. The good kind: I was falling fast. We kept kissing, his hand on the small of my back, my fingers curved around his neck. He pulled me on to his lap, and at that exact point someone noticed us from up at the house and shouted down in a teasing way, '*Allez!*'

The moment was over, and we pulled apart. I blushed. He stood up and wandered over to the pool, looking into the glowing water, which was lit up from below. Without fully thinking it through, I decided this was the moment to channel my best playful, mischievous energy, and walked over to him with a motive in mind. I was drunk but I was also giddy with first feelings, which can be even more intoxicating. And so I pushed Francesco with all my might. His hands had been in his pockets and he lost his balance easily, landing with a huge splash. I thought it would be funny; I thought it would be flirty.

Unfortunately, his brand new iPhone was in his pocket. Like I said, I didn't fully think it through. '*Putain*,' he swore loudly as his head resurfaced, reaching his hand up and out of the water, holding up his phone. His friends and Jasmine rushed down the grass from the house and Francesco threw it to them.

'Sorry!' I said in a high-pitched voice. My plan to be cute may have accidentally rebranded me as infuriating. One of his friends lifted me up and theatrically threw me into the pool on the count of three. I screamed as I flew through the air. Francesco swam towards me in an aggressive front crawl, water flying everywhere.

'I'm sorry, I'm sorry,' I said, not sure if he was seriously pissed off or about to burst into laughter; the expression on his face was one of deep concentration. But when he reached me, he grabbed my head and kissed me with complete fervour. We continued floating there, slowly spinning round, locking lips with the pool's spotlight on us, unbothered by the dozen or so people laughing at the edge of the pool.

It was that classic romcom formula: a misunderstanding, followed by an electrically charged making-up. Made all the more dramatic and romantic by the crowd of friends cheering you on. But in super-speed time.

When we got out we were both freezing, our wet clothes sticking to our skin and dripping with water. Francesco had been in jeans, and I was in a skirt and top. He once again took my hand and I followed him into the house and into his room. He locked the door. We looked at each other.

'I think we need a hot shower,' he said.

'Oh, do you?' I pulled a flirty expression and peeled off my clothes to reveal the bikini I had worn underneath.

'Definitely. I wouldn't want you to catch a cold.'

He had an en suite, and together we stepped under the stream of water, steam rising around us. The bikini didn't stay on for long.

Afterwards we went to lie on his bed, our skin still wet, tracing the outline of each other's bodies with the tips of our fingers.

Afterwards, he looked intently at me. 'This is only the beginning.'

I laughed. 'Maybe.'

When we rejoined the party, I discovered that Jasmine had enjoyed a romance of her own that night with one of Francesco's friends. They'd found a spare room and could only hope that it wasn't next to Francesco's parents.

Things only got stranger as the night turned to early morning. Francesco's friends warned me that he was a player, that he'd been in a ten-year relationship and they didn't know if he was ready for something more. It wasn't what I wanted to hear having just slept with the man, and it seemed odd his friends were warning me off him when they knew nothing about me. All things considered, I decided it was time to go home. Jasmine said she was ready to sleep too.

One of the guys said he would drive us, so we got our stuff together and I found Francesco to say goodbye. He was sad I was leaving and kissed me again, and when I told him what his friends had been saying, he was angry. I left him to deal with it. The journey back was not great – the friend had been drinking, and it was only when we were on the motorway I realised how dumb it had been to get in the car with him. I held tightly on to the seat, as if that would have somehow saved me in a crash. But we made it back, and Jasmine and I filed into the shared bathroom to have a shower side by side. When we came out, Gonçalo was there, brushing his teeth for the morning shift. He looked at us strangely. We said, 'Goodnight,' and slept until noon. The hangover in the heat the next day was one of my worst. My head and my body were sore, so I plunged myself into the salt water of the sea.

Francesco was right, though: that night did end up being just the beginning. We met once more in Nice and then again in Paris. And again. And again. We drank wine in trendy bars and watched the Eiffel Tower sparkle from his doorstep. If it wasn't my real life, I would have thought it was clichéd: but the city of love delivered the fairy-tale backdrop that felt exactly suited to us in that moment. It was grown-up and it was sultry and it was delicious. We were never serious; it was always a whirlwind. We knew one day I would leave to finish university and he would stay. But even after I left Paris, Francesco was still on my mind. For years afterwards, we'd call each other tipsy from one place or another, sending seductive photos and speaking in the way old lovers do.

That summer may have started with a heartbreak, but it ended with an enduring romance. And the best part wasn't that I'd found it possible to like someone again, but that if our story came to an end at some unforeseen point in the future, I would know how to deal with it. Okay, you can't always jump on a plane, but you can always fill your time with the things that make you feel like *you* again. You can surround yourself with good friends, you can dance like the morning will never come, you can eat pistachio gelato for dinner. And you can do it all with a broken heart, until one day you feel whole again.

Some things I've learned about meeting love interests in real life

- ♥ Delete the apps for at least a fortnight – you need the space to see what could be right in front of you.

- ♥ Delivering your number on a piece of paper and running away before they have time to read it is always an option if you can't bring yourself to ask someone out in person.

- ♥ Workplace romance is very much a thing – even if your job isn't as quirky as the body stand-ins in *Love Actually*.

- ♥ People from your hometown will have an unexplained appeal.

- ♥ Be tactical – sit at a larger table in the pub than you require. You never know who might ask if that chair is free.

- ♥ Keep your eyes peeled for Hugh Grants in bookshops.

- ♥ It's all about being approachable – two friends drinking at the bar is way better than a huge impenetrable group.

- ♥ Embrace being on the singles table at a wedding.

- ♥ *Clueless* told us stepbrothers are fair game. As if. They are not.

- ♥ Say yes to meeting that friend of a friend someone thinks you might like.

- ♥ Go on a ski holiday. Trust me.

- ♥ Quiz single friends on their favourite places to meet people. Pear Tree Café in Battersea Park on a sunny Thursday eve? Gold.

- ♥ Join a running club and swap Strava handles with anyone you think is intriguing.

7

27 TEQUILAS

Starring the one I'd like to forget

My first date with Jay nearly didn't happen. And that might have been better for both of us, considering what happened that night.

It started like any other routine app match. I scrolled through his profile. He knew what he was doing. Each pic was there to serve a purpose. *Oh, here is me in a suit at a wedding on my own* (I'm hot in high-res – come on, I know this matters). *Oh, here is me with a gaggle of friends who all happen to be shorter than me* (I'm a normal sociable being who can appear tall in the right circumstances). *Oh, here is me casually hanging out at Machu Picchu* (what can I say? I like to travel).

We'd been messaging for a couple of weeks, and we decided on an upcoming Thursday to meet in person. We hadn't formulated a plan, just set the day. As it drew closer, I texted him asking if seven was a good time and did he like the idea of tacos? It was a Tuesday morning when I messaged. Twenty-four hours passed and he hadn't replied: it was now the day before we were due to go out.

I was fed up with matches cancelling at the last minute with evidently fake and pathetic excuses, which only seemed to have got worse as I'd got older. First dates continue to be particularly bad for this: I guess it's because if you've never met before, it feels less like you're letting down an actual human being and more like you're just ignoring some virtual game on your phone. It's part of why people find online dating so draining– there is so much admin and an extremely high probability of disappointment.

This is exactly what I was saying to Hannah at 6pm the night before the date. We'd both been working from home and had just finished for the day, so were lying on our sides on my bed.

'I don't want to wait any longer. I'm going to message him,' I said.

'Yes, do it – you'll feel better after,' she agreed.

Together, we composed the message. We had done this many times. If you're a man who has received a text from me, there is a good chance that Hannah will have had some input in at least one of them. And vice versa – hi to all of Hannah's exes.

The message read:

> I'm guessing you don't want to meet anymore, but it would have been nice to let me know. Ciaoooo.

I was deep into my 'I'm done being messed around' era. I was over tiptoeing around to seem demure and was much more straight-talking.

He replied almost immediately. As my phone buzzed and the screen lit up, we both lunged for it. His message said:

> What? No, sorry, I just had a really busy day. I was about to reply. I'm still keen for tomorrow if you are? But if you don't want to, that's fine . . .

'Shit,' I said. 'Shit, shit. Why did you let me send that?'
'Oh my god. As if.' Hannah laughed.

On reflection, I had jumped to conclusions a little too fast. Hannah and I had egged each other on. He was his own person, not a reflection of some of the other men I had dated. Yes, it would have been nice for him to reply sooner, but maybe I should have at least waited it out before accusing him of ghosting. I'd lumped him in with all the terrible dating-app ghosters without giving him a chance. There's a danger, as we get older, in holding on to past experiences and pasting them on to someone new. Of course, a misunderstanding is one of the biggest plot devices in a romcom. Like when Jane thinks Kevin is only using her for his article in *27 Dresses*, or when Lara Jean breaks up with Peter because she thinks he was two-timing her in *To All the Boys I've Loved Before*. It adds a drama and intensity that only brings our lovers closer together – though the same can't always be true in real life. There's a danger, too, in holding out for this, in waiting to be proved wrong, when sometimes the feeling in our gut is the cold, hard truth.

But this time, I actually had been wrong.

We went downstairs to show Shreya the exchange. 'Is there any way of saving this? Or does he already think I'm a weirdo?'

'Ciaoooo,' said Shreya.

'Ciao ciao,' said Hannah.

'Why did you decide to end the message with "Ciao"?' asked Shreya.

'I don't know. I wrote it without thinking too much. Hannah said it was a good message!' I looked at Hannah.

She shrugged.

'I guess maybe I thought it conveyed that I wasn't going to take any bullshit, but also that I am being somewhat playful and light-hearted?' I said. 'An "I don't really care" sort of vibe?'

'Ha, well, I hate to break it to you, but the message reads exactly like you did care, and now you're pissed off,' Shreya said.

'Stopppp. Stop. Okay, I can see now it comes across as sarcastic. Okay, maybe more than that. Maybe I sound like an exasperated woman who found out her scumbag boyfriend has cheated and thinks she deserves more? I honestly didn't think he would reply, but now I feel like an idiot. I've messed it up before I've even gone on the bloody date.'

'It's fine,' said Hannah, ever the calmer out of us three. 'Just reply with something normal, and five minutes into the date you'll both have forgotten this ever happened.'

'Okay, thank you,' I said.

'And breathe,' said Hannah.

I managed to style it out, and so we decided to meet as planned the next evening. Hannah was right. It was easy, breezy. Admittedly, part of the reason I felt so relaxed was that I had drunk a few glasses of Prosecco in the office with my colleagues before arriving.

Jay was friendly, intelligent, interesting. Dark hair, average height, an architect. He'd lived in the US for a number of years and loved running and impressionist art and octopuses – as an animal, not to eat. He was vegetarian. Neither of us mentioned the word 'ciao'. The conversation rolled seamlessly from one topic to another.

We drank a bottle of red wine quicker than intended with guacamole and chips. When the waiter asked if we wanted anything more to drink, I looked at Jay. 'Margaritas?'

'Margaritas,' he replied.

I have since learned that drinking to the point of drunkenness on a first date isn't the best indicator of chemistry: how can you tell if what you have is real or just lust fuelled by tequila? This may sound obvious, but it took me well into my twenties to consciously learn.

When he later asked if I wanted to go for a nightcap at his place, I didn't hesitate.

The question of when to sleep with someone for the first time is one that is fraught with differing opinions. Some of my friends insist that you shouldn't do anything more than kiss until you've met each other at least three times. I'm pretty sure this is romcom induced. There's a lot of internalised misogyny in the genre, a sense that women can't expect to be seen as anything other than a sexual object if they 'offer' themselves up too soon. I hate this framing; it implies it's the woman's fault that she is sexualised.

Others think the second date is the perfect moment. You have assessed they aren't a serial killer (as much as you ever can) and you haven't invested too much time if you're about to find out there is not an ounce of sexual chemistry.

I've changed my mind several times about whether you should wait or not. I've slept with people on the night I met them and gone on to have great love stories. I've waited for five or six dates, only to never see them again. I've landed here: do what feels right. If you sleep with them 'too early' and they like you less because of that, then they are the problem and you're lucky to have escaped. If you sleep with them 'too late' and they get impatient, then again, they are the problem and you're lucky to have escaped.

Anyway, on this particular night, I was having fun and I wasn't ready for the evening to end. I was open to the idea of a nightcap, and I would decide whether I wanted anything more once I was plumped on his sofa.

We got an Uber because he had cycled to the restaurant and wouldn't have been able to bring his bike on the tube. It was only when we were in the car, heading eastwards through stop-and-start traffic, that I realised how drunk I was. That there was a possibility I would need to be sick and, given that I was in a cab, this was not an option. I pressed the button to roll down the window and stuck my head out like a little puppy dog. Except not like a puppy dog, because I did not look cute.

The driver noticed immediately. 'Is she okay?'

Jay looked at me. 'Um, are you okay?'

'Yeah, totally fine. Just a little tipsier than expected, but the cold air is helping.'

'Is she going to be sick?' asked the driver.

'You can ask me, I can hear you. I'm not going to be sick. I'm fine. Fiiiine.'

I wasn't really fine, though, and the drive was far longer than I had anticipated. 'Where do you live again? How much further is it?' I asked meekly, sure that if I could see my face in a mirror, I might notice I was turning a funny colour.

'Haggerston – it's just five more minutes. Are you sure you're okay?'

'Yes. I just can't talk.' We sat in silence for what felt like five years instead of five minutes. I was doing everything I could to prevent myself from being sick. I tried counting to ten. I tried closing my eyes, opening my eyes. Sticking my head further out of the window, pulling it back in. I knew, though, that my attempts to hold back the proverbial tide were all pointless; it was simply a question of time. We needed to get to his asap.

And then suddenly we were there. We got out of the car, and being on my own two feet made me feel miraculously better. Luck was on my side. I forgot about feeling sick, distracted by my new surroundings. Jay lived in this incredible warehouse with warren-like tunnels leading us this way and that before going up some industrial stairs into his apartment proper.

The shared living space was huge, with tall ceilings and cool furniture and funky art and lots of bikes on the walls. We stayed there for a while before making our way to his bedroom, which you needed to climb up a wooden ladder to get to. For a south-west London girl, it felt extremely edgy.

Once we were in his room, we started to fool around, and before long it had escalated into sex. His bed was a mattress on the floor – please, lord, tell me why do so many thirty-something men insist on this? And why do they then try to pass it off as an interior design choice? Same goes for having only one pillow. Sort it out.

I was on top and then, out of nowhere, I vomited on him, on

myself, and on the bed. Okay, not totally out of nowhere, but I hadn't felt like I needed to be sick since stepping out of the car, otherwise I might have enjoyed a discreet tactical chunder. Sadly, there was no prior warning, no chance to aim for a bin. If it had been a Farrow & Ball colour, they might have named it 'Red Wine Reborn'.

'Oh, fuck. I am so, so sorry,' I half-whispered, half-squealed.

He looked at me: 'It's . . . okay?'

'Oh my god. This is horrifically embarrassing. I haven't been sick from drinking in a long time, and obviously never on someone else,' I gabbled.

He got up and started to strip the bed, first the pillowcase and then the sheets, which required me to get up and stand awkwardly, looming over him on the floor. I was naked and cold and covered in my own sick; I wanted to shrivel up and disappear.

'You may want to go use the shower downstairs,' he said, without turning around.

I climbed carefully down the ladder to his shared loo, trying not to let any of the sick drip off on to any more surfaces and hoping none of his housemates would decide to relieve themselves at this exact moment. I locked the door as soon as I was inside, and spun round to catch a glimpse of myself in the larger-than-I-would-have-wished-for-in-that-moment mirror. Sick had clumped my hair together into lumpy stalactites and splattered across my bosom, which was still rosy red from the heaving passion of the sex I had been having moments before. And I thought 'Ciaoooo' had been embarrassing.

When I returned upstairs, Jay was scrubbing ferociously at the mattress with stain remover and a dishcloth. He was using the full force of his body, and his bare bottom was bopping up and down. If it wasn't still horrifically, horrendously humiliating, it would have been funny.

Jay was sweet about it, handling it better than most would have. He could see how embarrassed I was and didn't want to make it any worse. Once we'd put fresh sheets on and crawled under the clean covers, he checked that I was okay, asked if I wanted a glass of water, told me not to worry. Then he asked in a quiet voice if I had been too drunk to decide whether to have sex. That thought hadn't crossed my mind, but I could understand why it might be consuming him. I told him that I had known what I was doing, just not how sick I was about to be. And that was the truth, but I was glad that he had asked.

We woke up early the next morning, with the sound of rain on his skylight and with a whiff of my mistake. I couldn't wait to get out of there, partly because my embarrassment hung even heavier in the light of day, partly because I couldn't wait to call my sister Kate and retell the story so she could share in my shame. She would find a way to make me feel better. To spin the story to make me seem like less of an idiot. Or, more likely, she'd tell me I *am* an idiot but a lovable one.

I had the day off, but Jay was cycling into work. We got dressed and he gathered the pile of vomit-covered sheets in the corner of the room and shoved them into a black plastic bin bag.

'Are you not going to wash them?'

'No,' he said.

I didn't blame him for not wanting to ever have to think about this again. 'I'm happy to give you some money for new sheets. It's the least I can do,' I offered.

'You don't have to do that; it's not like you did it on purpose. At least, I hope not.' He was trying to make light of the situation. I appreciated it.

'I just really thought you needed some new sheets?' I joked weakly. 'Please, let me pay.'

On the way out, he threw the bin bag dramatically up into the air and into a dumpster. I expected a large crash, but instead there was an anticlimactic muffled thud. It was just sheets and sick, after all.

Jay gave me a quick kiss goodbye before pedalling off. He did send me his bank details when I pestered him, and I did send some money. It made me feel marginally better.

Later that day, I remembered that the same thing had happened to my friend Keshet. I called her to tell her about it, and she reassured me that she had felt equally embarrassed, but it hadn't stopped the man in question asking her on a second date.

'He did *not* ask you on a second date? After you were sick on him?' I asked.

'He did. There's nothing to say that Jay won't too. In fact, I think he will.' It reminded me of the scene in *How to Lose a Guy in 10 Days* when Andie's friend Michelle says, 'No. No guy would go running from you, Andie. You could barf all over him and he'd say, "Do it again."' She may have been exaggerating, but it turns out she was probably right – and so was Keshet.

Jay didn't wait long before suggesting we go to a trendy bakery-meets-pasta-restaurant somewhere in east London, not far from his home. He was willing to risk ending up back at his again.

When the waitress asked us what we wanted to drink, I made a joke that I was rationing myself to one glass of wine. Jay said, 'We'll have the bottle.'

So I guess the lesson is that if they like you, it's going to take more than a little (okay, a lot of) sick to put them off. Not to mention that it's silly to get so hung up on scrutinising your every move: real chemistry can't be contrived through workshopped messages. It's even more powerful than projectile vomit.

Now, whenever it's time to say goodbye to a romantic interest, Hannah, Shreya and I all scream in silly unison: 'Ciaooooo.'

Some things I've learned about dating

♥ Spontaneous first dates are often the best.

♥ You'll need nicknames to keep your friends up to date: Peanut Butter Boy, No-bed Man, and Angel Gabriel.

♥ If you get the feeling they are hiding something from you, the thing they are hiding is very unlikely to be the fact that they're a prince of a far-flung country.

♥ Only assholes consider taking yourself too seriously a bad thing.

♥ When anyone says there are plenty of fish in the sea, they're lying. It's full of trash and all the fish are dying.

♥ Yes, that's from a TikTok, one of the hundreds that you will constantly send to your single friends.

♥ Be wary of anyone who love-bombs you.

♥ You'll meet people through dating you would never come across in your normal social circle, and you'll be happier for it.

♥ Don't trust men with single-syllable names: Zane, Joe, Brad.

♥ If you tell someone you've had a threesome and they become obsessed with it, it says more about them than you.

♥ Kiss in the rain every chance you get. It actually is just as romantic as in the films.

- Even more romantic is a long-awaited kiss at the very top of a Ferris wheel. Just ask the leads of *Love, Simon*.

- The same is probably true of hearing someone shout your name as they run through an airport, but sadly no one does this in real life.

- As soon as you start composing your WhatsApps in the Notes app before sending them, it's the beginning of the end.

- There are far fewer handsome widowers in your hometown than Hallmark movies would have you believe.

- The good-butterfly feeling is addictive.

- Yas in *Rye Lane* is absolutely right: you only want to date people who wave enthusiastically at boats.

- Treat yourself (and your dates) with kindness.

- Celebrate the first shoots of excitement and intrigue when they arrive. They may not happen every time, and therein lies their wonder.

8

HE'S JUST NOT THAT INTO ME

Starring the one I reconnected with from school

There are certain situations that give a halo effect to otherwise ordinary men – and meeting someone as an adult whom you once went to school with is one of them. I'm not sure I ever expected to fall for so many men from Swindon, but here we are.

There was a friend's tall older brother, who had a kind face and ginger beard, who I spotted in a club at university while I was dressed as a nymph. We shared a kiss, and my other friends couldn't understand my excitement. We did end up dating for a couple of months (it included cinema dates with his dad and blueberry pancakes with my mum) but it never really got off the ground.

Then there was the man I'd once had French lessons with. Our class was small, and the two of us became close when we did the French exchange two years in a row. We messaged on and off, met one time in Paris when we were both studying in France, and then, nearly a decade later, he messaged me out of the blue to see if I wanted to meet. The attraction was still there, but it was a casual daytime encounter and it didn't end up going anywhere. We exchanged a few messages that were on the cusp of sexy, but he moved to Canada shortly after.

And then there was Dan Smith. I hadn't really noticed him during school, but somehow he became a season regular when I was in my twenties. Okay, for a little bit of my thirties too. But no more!

So please heed my warning and ask yourself, do you really have chemistry or did you have chemistry lessons together aged sixteen? Of course, it is possible to reconnect with someone from school and for it to be spellbindingly right. I have a friend who recently married someone we thought of as one of the bad boys at sixth form, and it just works. There's my colleague who dated her now-partner for several weeks before they realised they'd gone to the same primary school and are in a class picture together. And we can't forget that it worked for Jenna and Matty in *13 Going on 30* – the lesson there being that it took growing up for her to realise what she'd been missing out on as a kid.

But these are the exceptions. For the most part, the halo effect wears off after a time, and suddenly you aren't sure if you would even be seeing each other if it weren't for the common denominator of having once shared a school. This isn't to say they aren't attractive, but just that the thing tying you together isn't as binding as you thought.

So, where did it all begin with Dan? Certainly not at school. If I really concentrate, I can just about picture him with his soft brunette hair. He'd sit at the back of the classroom, cracking jokes with the confidence of someone who knows they will get top marks even if they don't pay full attention. Apparently he gave me a lift home once, but I can't remember it. The only message I received from him while at school was a list of song suggestions for the Year 13 Winter Ball that I was organising in my role as Head Girl.

Hiiii Elizabeth :)

> i typed up those requests we got back from asking people, we tried to keep them sensible and mainstream so everyone will be happy :L and if the guy doesn't have some of them, then we'll bring in a CD ;)

The list transports me back to 2010 ... We're talking 'Only Girl' by Rihanna (the Bimbo Jones Club Mix – an important clarification here from Dan) and 'Barbra Streisand' by Duck Sauce. Plus early 2000s hits like 'All the Small Things' by Blink-182, 'Mr Brightside' by The Killers and 'Chelsea Dagger' by The Fratellis. Listening to these songs now makes me sentimental. I can see a younger me in a short, tight dress and heels bopping around the club, thinking Swindon Bushwhackers was the height of cool. (It wasn't.)

After six years of having gone our separate ways, Dan made contact. I was working and living in London at the time, but the catalyst for our reconnection was a place further away: Thailand. We were both on holiday there when I received his Facebook message:

> Lizzie are you in Chiang Mai at the moment

He'd seen an Instagram post of mine (featuring, of course, dirty trainers, harem pants and an elephant) and taken it as his opportunity. This technique didn't have a name back then, but now I'd say without hesitation that he was very clearly sliding into my DMs.

I'd already moved south for the spectacular sunsets and night-life of the islands, but we chatted for a while about our onward plans and the possibility of where our paths might cross. Maybe Koh Pha-ngan for the Full Moon Party? Maybe Koh Tao for diving or snorkelling?

He also hinted that he would be moving to London when he

got back from the trip, saying, 'I'm certain I'll be seeing you soon in London.' A bold statement considering we weren't friends and hadn't hung out since school. I assumed he had to be flirting with me, but couldn't quite put my finger on what he was looking for. I was intrigued rather than interested.

As it turned out, our paths never crossed in Asia, in part because his foot got infected thanks to a cut he didn't take care of and he had to spend a few days in hospital recovering before he could walk again. He took it in his stride, a funny story to recount at parties. But he didn't restart the conversation when he arrived home, and I quickly forgot about the whole exchange.

Six weeks or so later, he popped up on Bumble and – ping – we matched.

I sent the first message:

> Haha Dan Smith has moved to london.

If the fact I full-named him seems odd, know that this is always how I have referred to him, even when it would have been obvious to my friends and family who I was talking about. Perhaps it is a hangover from school, where there were multiple Dans. But over the various iterations of our relationship, he never became just Dan to me.

He replied:

> Ha ha it's so funny. I moved here on Wednesday and you were like the second person who popped up. How are your Thailand blues

Please note the lack of a question mark. He rarely used them – not then, not years later. Perhaps he has never thought about it, but I can't help but wonder if this was a tactic to seem less interested. Especially as I have seen many flames since also avoid punctuation at all costs. My messages are usually littered with exclamation marks, yet sometimes I've found myself dropping them when chatting to a boy in an effort to match their energy like a desperate idiot.

It's important to remember I'm part of the first generation to have dated in the era of non-stop, internet-enabled communication. I was raised on MSN, then graduated to WhatsApp via Facebook Messenger and iMessages. And so, deep down, I know misplaced punctuation is no 'accident'. The errors and gaps often speak a thousand words. My peers and I are masters of communicating tone and intention through the placement, misplacement or deliberate non-placement of punctuation, capitalisation and more.

The conversation continued like a strange dance, swirling around each other but never quite meeting in the middle. There were questions about weekend plans, responses about not much on, but nothing ever as forward as saying, 'Let's hang out.' We'd matched on an app – so surely we knew there was some interest on both sides – but we couldn't seem to navigate moving from not-really-friends to something more. Who would make the first move?

Dan decided on the baby step of sweeping us into voice-note territory.

I recorded back: 'It's so funny to hear your voice, I probably haven't seen you in millions of years.'

He replied with a characteristic chortle: 'Literally yours too, I can't believe it.' He added, 'I feel like being at university might have diluted your accent a little bit.'

We carried on like this for two months, discussing everything from work trials and tribulations to anecdotes from nights out and weekend travels. I mocked him for his formal language: who uses the term 'daily deliverables' with someone you're trying to pursue? Even if you are talking about your job?

But the voice notes also endeared him to me. He was both

smart and silly in the way he expressed himself and he made me laugh. His voice was higher pitched than I remembered, but I liked it – compared with the texts, he sounded far more engaged and excited. Then finally, after two months of chatting, he wrote:

> You should come and visit mine and Charlie's place. At least it's south of the river.

Charlie is another school friend, who had been friends with Dan for years so they had moved in together.

My heart beat a little faster. I said:

> Invite me round.

He suggested we ask some other Swindon pals, and I was disappointed he was transforming it into a group event. Even then, we failed to find a date we were both free in the near vicinity and soon the messages trickled out – other than a few on the bleak, grey November day Trump was elected:

> Are you watching this?!

> I can't believe this.

In February, Charlie invited me to dinner:

> I've asked Zoë too, and there should be a couple of others. Dan will be there of course.

Zoë and I had become friends during sixth form and she also knew the boys; we had drifted apart during university, but when we became two of the only women in our year to move to London we had reconnected. She's thoughtful, kind, and loyal – and is equally as happy on an unplanned Big Night Out as a long walk in Richmond Park. Not to mention we've both been single on and off for most of our time since school, so we always have dating stories to exchange. In a way, knowing Dan brought us closer together. She's the one woman in my inner orbit who knows him from our teenage days like I do, and she was there for many of our early encounters in London – the first of which was that night.

Now remember, by this point, Dan and I hadn't exchanged so much as a 'Hi' for months, so I was convinced I had read the situation all wrong. Okay, I spent a little longer than usual choosing my outfit that afternoon, but that was mainly to feel confident when I walked into the room. I didn't think anything like a kiss was on the cards; it was more likely he'd pretend that the last time we'd chatted was in our lacklustre common room or waiting for the loo at the Leavers' Ball. He either had grown bored of our voice notes, decided I wasn't right for him or met someone new. That's what I told myself as I looked in the mirror before heading out the door.

On the way from the tube to their higgedly-piggedly flat, swaddled in coats and bags clinking, I gave Zoë the necessary details. Perhaps her outside perspective would give her the ability to suss the situ. It was thirty minutes or so after sunset, the sky a wonderful luminescent indigo.

'So, when I was in Thailand last year, Dan messaged me, and then we matched on an app in London, and then we sent all these voice notes back and forth.'

She smiled. 'So what do you think will happen tonight?'

'No, no, it's not like that – or at least, I don't think it is. I thought we might go on a date, but then he just went radio silent. So. Who. Knows.'

Zoë didn't hesitate. 'Leave it to me, I'll find out what's going on.'

'But what if it's awkward?' I squealed.

'It won't be. They wouldn't have invited us otherwise.'

She was right, of course – and, as I would learn over the years,

Dan and Charlie are excellent hosts when it comes to dinner parties. They know precisely the right number of people to invite (circa six, as we were that night), can turn out a decent meal with minimum fuss, and always have games and good music ready to go. Oh, and there's always a lot of booze – gin and tonics to start, red wine to follow, and then who knows what. On reflection, there's always more women than men too, and I'm not entirely convinced this isn't intentional. They like to have the odds in their favour.

That night was no exception. They both greeted us at the door, faces beaming, the smell of something cosy and delicious already wafting through from the tiny kitchen.

'Thanks so much for coming, we'll give you the grand tour,' said Charlie. 'But first, coats! Zoë, you can put yours in my room. Lizzie, Dan will take yours.' I swear I could see a smirk on his face, a hint of a conversation that had taken place before we had arrived. It was a weirdly bold move, especially given how tentative Dan had been up until this point. It was the first sign that Dan might still be interested – why else would they put our coats in separate rooms? Why would they put the coats anywhere at all? It's not like this was a huge house party, or a mansion in the countryside. And yet, Charlie denies it to this day. He says it was an offhand comment, and it meant nothing. I still don't believe him.

Our whirlwind tour done, we moved into the living room, where we met friends of Dan's from his time spent living in Singapore. For dinner, Charlie had cooked six individual chicken pies, with the finishing touch of our initials in pastry on top. They'd even prepared a cheese board (courtesy of Aldi's finest selection) for dessert.

We were full and tipsy and playful, and so someone threw out a *Twister* mat and we tried to play. I say 'tried' as we were all quite drunk, so everybody fell over within the first minute. There was a palpable sexual tension as I got entangled with Dan on the mat, falling with a thud to the floor. Soon we were dancing, the six of us

swirling around salsa-style to Latin American hits. I think I peaked
when Shakira's 'Hips Don't Lie' came on. 'Peaked' meaning that I
was having the time of my life, not that I looked sexy in any way. I
have never been able to feel the rhythm or remember lyrics, so I just
have to accept dancing isn't something I look great doing.

At one point we ran out of wine, although I am not quite sure
how this was possible based on the stock they had at the beginning of the evening. Zoë and Dan headed to the shop while I
helped Charlie clear up. When Zoë reappeared twenty minutes
later, she gave me a sneaky thumbs-up. I looked at her quizzically.
She came closer and whispered: 'I asked him and he's definitely,
maybe, interested.'

'What do you mean?'

'Well, he didn't categorically *say* he was, but he hinted at it.
And I could just tell.'

I woke up the next morning to the sound of the radio announcing that *La La Land* had been falsely declared the winner at the
Oscars instead of *Moonlight*. It was a surreal moment, and it took
me a minute or two to collect my thoughts and realise it wasn't a
joke. Then I rolled over to see Dan and his room, and everything
began to feel even more surreal.

'Morning,' I said meekly.

'Morning,' he replied and gave me a sloppy kiss. 'I am definitely working from home today.' Then he rolled over and switched
off the radio with his outstretched arm in one smooth movement.

I didn't have that option and it was already 8am, so I had no
choice but to go straight into work at my magazine job. I got up
and gathered my things while he stayed in bed, then he showed
me to the door. The atmosphere wasn't awkward, but we weren't
totally at ease either.

On my way to the tube, I saw that I had already received a text
from Zoë, who had left around midnight to catch the last train;
meanwhile, I hadn't gone to bed until nearly 3am.

Omg I feel horrific. Hope you're okay. How was the rest of your night?

I'm just leaving now.

Hahahaha amazing. Any goss?

I mean your matchmaking skills

Did they work?

Oh my god can't believe that happened. Yup.

Omg tell me

Was spooning Dan Smith when you texted me lol. I'll call you at lunch or later

I think it's fair to say I wasn't very productive that day: a hangover and a serious lack of sleep did not work in my favour. One colleague commented on how nice I looked, which made me smile considering I was wearing dirty clothes and the crumbs of yesterday's make-up. Clearly my aura was giving off confidence from the antics of the night before.

When I finally got home after what felt like an eternity of a day, I called Zoë to go over every minute detail, from ringing the doorbell to the goodbye kiss.

I think half the fun of a new romantic interest is the debrief call you get to have with a close friend the next day. Dissecting what they said, cackling at embarrassing moments and sharing the heady rush of feelings you're processing. It's what bonds me and my friends together. If I get an incoming call the day after a friend has been on a date, I know to drop everything and prepare for a story. It might be a silly one, or a serious one, or a dear-god-how-do-I-carry-on-doing-this one – it's hard to tell before you answer the call, but all of them bring us closer for one reason or another. Like when Alice rang me to say, 'And then, just as I was straightening my hair on the floor after a shower, he said, "I can call you my girlfriend, right?" He just said it like that, so casually. I thought my heart might explode'. Or when Nick told me, 'We were walking in Bloomsbury and then he said he knew a secret spot, and he took me through this unmarked door, up a fire escape and suddenly we were on a rooftop looking out over the city. We were just rolling around making out and it was sunset. Is this dating in London?!' Or Zoë, admitting, 'It happened again with that guy, but he's still a twat and I'm still not sure why I keep going back to him.'

The difference was that this time, Zoë had actually been there and so it wasn't just my perspective but more of a 360-view of the whole night. I got her take on particular vignettes and eaves-dropped on moments I hadn't been part of, and we laugh-cried together at silly things the boys had done. We giggled about the coats, discussed if there had been any energy between her and Charlie (deciding that there had not), and of course we talked about Dan Smith. How Zoë had been so obvious in her hints that he should make a move; how he'd given me a hickey and thank god I'd brought a scarf with me to wear at work; how we'd ended up having sex; what he'd texted since and whether I thought I would see him again.

But this was not the start of a great fiery love story; it was the beginning of something messy and complicated and tepid, where neither of us seemed to choose each other but somehow we kept ending up together.

Over the coming months, I saw Dan a smattering of times, but nearly always in a group setting. More dinner parties, pub trips, that sort of thing. There was also a house party at mine a few weeks later where we both kissed other people: me, a beardy man who was a friend of a friend; him, a work pal of Zoë's. I was angry and had no right to be. I don't really know why I kissed the other boy, other than because I was drunk and liked the attention. And maybe I thought it would make Dan jealous.

Later, he tried to kiss me in the kitchen surrounded by a gaggle of people (including both the people we had each already snogged). I told him he had messed up and it was time for him to leave, but he refused. He said he would go upstairs to my bed and wait for me there. I let him go, but continued for hours at the party before eventually returning to my room. I creaked open the door to reveal Dan Smith fast asleep in the corner of my bed near the window, face smushed up against the pillow. In that moment, I forgave him. I crawled in beside him and fell asleep. In the morning, we kissed and slept together again.

We went downstairs to find someone's shoe in the punch bowl and snuck out for brunch – sorry to my housemates who did most (read: all) of the cleaning. Later, Zoë called me to tell me she had fallen asleep in the attic with no memory of why she'd decided to kip there.

'Was anyone with you? A boy, perhaps?'

'No, I wish.' She laughed.

Dan Smith and I did message on and off, but reading our conversation back now is embarrassing for me. He would take a while to reply, and I was always the one pushing it forward when I should have let it be. The phrase, 'If he wanted to, he would,' comes to mind. At first it felt like neither of us were all in, and we kept getting pulled together by chance, but as time went on I did want to properly try out the idea of us. It wasn't that I wanted a serious relationship with him – it was too early to decide that – but I wanted to date him. And I wanted him to want to date me.

We did break the group-setting pattern once to spend time just the two of us – the night we stayed at a five-star hotel, The Langham. My job has often included the perk of getting to sleep in beautiful hotels, but until this point I had only visited them alone or with friends or family. Never with someone I was seeing, someone I fancied.

I wrote:

> Dan Smith, I have a proposition for you. I've got a few hotel reviews for work coming up. I was thinking it could be potentially quite fun if you joined me on one. But it's likely to be a week night and I know you have an early bed time, so no worries if not your thing.

I was giving him a get-out clause before I'd even let him reply. He said:

> Oh Lizzie. Absolutely, I would love to, how exciting. I don't have an early bed time when I have a day bag pre-packed, so it's all good. That sounds fabulous.

His reply was overwhelmingly positive, but was it because he'd be spending time with me? Or was it the night in the fancy hotel? I'm going to be generous and say a combination of the two.

I arrived before Dan, picking up some nice underwear from the Big Topshop on Oxford Street [RIP] on my way, after remembering I'd only packed granny panties. I know now the cheaper option would have just been to take them off and play it off as a move.

The suite was gorgeous: a princess-and-the-pea-style bed and a marble bathroom with a glorious tub.

The phone rang and I answered; it was reception.

'Hello, Ms Frainier, I have Dan Smith for you.' It sounded so ridiculous, but I loved hearing it.

'Send him up,' I replied in my poshest and most powerful voice. I hoped that he could hear me through the receiver. I was both nervous and excited as I waited for him to arrive. The nature of my job really has afforded me many moments that seem like the backdrop to a romcom. I mean, there's always a fancy hotel scene, right? Ahem, Julia Roberts in *Notting Hill*.

I opened the door to reveal Dan Smith in a smart shirt, grinning from ear to ear. 'Helloooo,' he said in a silly voice.

'Champagne?' I asked.

We chatted and poked fun at each other before dinner, where he ordered the most expensive thing on the menu knowing it was free, a lobster dish with silky tortellini. The swish setting and the fact we had both dressed up made me feel like we were playing at being proper adults. It was both highly grown-up and refined, and sexy as hell. That evening we had a decadent bath in the cavernous tub together, flutes of fizz in hands – I even have a photo of him, the bubbles covering just enough.

Our suite gave us access to the breakfast lounge, which was filled with business people getting ready for the day. We chose from the buffet and sat opposite each other, him reading the *Financial Times*, me sipping at my tea. I couldn't help but laugh, looking at him reading about the markets before a day in the office: had we fast-forwarded twenty years and become a married power couple?

The next few years of our story are blank: pretty much right after this, he moved to Buenos Aires for a master's degree and met an Argentinian woman, who even moved to London with him later. Charlie was the one to fill me in over espresso martinis at 1am; he said it in a generous way, a casual comment that gave me the info but was cautious not to imply he thought it might affect me.

My friendship with Dan did continue and grow, though; he attended my birthday parties, we danced in the streets to reggaeton at Notting Hill Carnival, we went on a bike ride back in Wiltshire, and he even came to see me in a local play I was in. Looking back now, his relationship gave us the opportunity to know each other in a platonic way, to see that we had something beyond the lust and attraction.

I remember the moment I found out he was single again very clearly; I had moved on and didn't think we would ever have a renaissance. And yet my stepdad, Matthew, thought differently. One evening over dinner with my mum, he said, 'Oh we ran into your friend, Charlie, and he told us Dan Smith and his girlfriend have broken up. Just thought I'd let you know.'

I choked on my wine. 'What's that supposed to mean?'

'Oh, nothing.' Matthew smiled.

It wasn't until Christmas that I saw Dan again, now several months out of his relationship. We went for a misty walk through damp fields on Boxing Day with Charlie and more of their friends before hopping from village pub to village pub. The group peeled away until it was just me, Charlie and Dan – we decided to prolong the evening by heading into Swindon's old town for a techno night. Yes, you read that right. And yes, it was as bizarre as it sounds.

I could feel Dan flirting with me again at the bar and on the dance floor for the first time in nearly five years, but I had just returned from my New York flat-swap *Holiday* trip where I had met Evan, and so my heart was not open to Dan. To me, he was still just a friend. Once again, I was intrigued but not interested.

A month or so later, Dan commented on an Instagram post of mine of a series of bathtubs:

> Very nice! Still prefer the fave from 2016 though.

I was sitting in my living room when I received the notification. I laughed out loud. 'Oh my god,' I muttered.

'What?' Hannah asked.

'Look at this.' I held out my phone.

She took a minute to read the message and then also started laughing, somewhat manically. 'That is such bold flirting,' she said.

'Show me,' chimed our new housemate Dhara, who came over to the sofas from where she was stirring something on the stove. 'Oh wow,' she said.

'I can't believe he's written that for all the world to see,' I said. 'Also, not to be a perfectionist, but the bath we shared was in 2017.'

'Come on, Dan,' joked Hannah.

'Should I message him?'

'Yes,' said Dhara.

I sent him a WhatsApp:

> The 2016 bath – not sure I remember that one?

He replied:

> Hahaha. Sure you do. It's your best pic of a bath in a hotel for sure

The texting continued, but in classic Dan Smith style he did not invite me on a date. Of course, I didn't ask him on one either. The next time we saw each other was my birthday in mid-February. By this time, things with Evan had fizzled and I was seeking romantic connection once again.

I made slow-cooked beef tacos, harissa cauliflower, refried beans and more. I put Hannah on guacamole duty, and Dhara in charge of the pickled onions. There was a rum punch and my new favourite drink – tequila and tonic with a slice of grapefruit and a sprig of rosemary. Dan arrived late, and I noticed there was a zingy feeling in my stomach, an anticipation of what might happen when we were in the same room again. I realised I would be disillusioned if he bailed at the last moment.

I was happy to be surrounded by friends, cooking and hosting. It was lovely to see multiple iterations of housemates all together too: Jess and Hannah from the early days, and now Shreya and

Dhara. Nick brought moreish home-made cookies à la Ravneet Gill, and Alina a pair of Himalayan salt shot glasses. Soon we were all partaking in the tequila, and I cut my finger when I got overexcited about the slicing of the limes. Dan stayed close to me for much of the evening, touching my back gently, helping me with a plaster on my little finger, encouraging other guests to partake in the shots. And at one point, we disappeared upstairs. When we returned to the living room, Nick cheered. I laughed and said, 'Shh, nothing happened.' They knew me too well to believe me.

The party ended at around 1am and Dan stayed over. It was never a question, he just did. In the morning, he said, 'It's kind of surreal to be here again.' I still had the same room from all those years ago. Yes, some of the decorations had changed, my sheets were different, but it was, in essence, the same. I suppose you could say something similar about us – we were five years older, with different jobs, different bodies and different hearts. But we were, in essence, the same. We laughed so much that after he left, my housemates asked what on earth was so funny. But there wasn't anything in particular; it was just the way we were with each other.

This time I decided to be more forward: I was no longer that twenty-four-year-old who couldn't ask a man on a date.

I asked if he wanted to do something soon, or if he wanted another five-year hiatus.

He replied:

> How about tomorrow. Is that too soon were you thinking more like 2.5 years

> I can make an exception.

We met in Peckham. He had bought a flat nearby and had suggested we meet at a cocktail bar.

It was a Sunday, and I spent the afternoon having brunch at a friend's in Streatham – Alina, of the infamous Himalayan salt shot glasses. She's one of my Shamrock girls – the five of us had individual friendships at university, but only really bonded as a group after moving to London. We began to meet once a month for dinner (sometimes out, sometimes one of us would cook) and before long we booked a trip to Dublin (hence, Shamrock). We're all on different career paths (from art and marketing to buying and international relations), but we all hype each other up. The other four have been in relationships for years – two are married now – but they've always been there for me through the ups and downs of dating. That day, we talked about Dan Smith and the fact we were finally going on a date.

Beth said, 'I really have a good feeling about this. I like him.' Beth had met him at my birthdays, and also when we'd danced at Notting Hill Carnival.

Tara chimed in. 'He works at the same place as me! Let me look him up on our intranet!'

I replied: 'Okay – let's see how the first date goes.'

And it was a date, a proper date. We drank swish cocktails in a tucked-away corner, the lively Irish music floating in from the front of the bar. He'd put on nice shoes and a shirt, and there was a tangible energy between us. Except that we already knew each other, so there was none of the 'How many siblings do you have?' chat. We could dive straight in.

We went for dinner, and afterwards he didn't invite me back – he just started walking in the direction of his flat, his hand locked around mine.

'Excuse me, are you going to invite me over or just walk me in the direction of your house? I could be planning on getting the tube home for all you know.' I smirked.

'But you're not.' He squeezed my hand.

'You don't know that.' I squeezed back.

'I do.'

We fell into his bed and into each other's arms. The next morning, we both left for work with a hug and kiss.

And then, nothing.

I had been the one to finally suggest a date, so I felt it was his turn to text me – I wasn't going to make the first move again. He didn't message that day. That week. That month. I assumed it was done.

Until six whole months later, when I received a screenshot of my Hinge profile from his phone that read 'Most Compatible'. In between, we'd had no contact at all, not even as friends.

His message read:

> It's meant to be, Lizzie

I replied with something curt. I was no longer interested in this behaviour. It was boring.

Until a month later, when I'd had several coconuts spiked with rum at Notting Hill Carnival, and I sent a sexy photo of me in a short, sparkly dress. The place and the music and the parades will always remind me of him, and I couldn't help myself. I then sent a message to say:

> Pls ignore the last photo.

He said:

> I don't think I am capable of ignoring that, Lizzie. It's a very sexy photo you cant expect me to be able to delete it from my memory.

I didn't reply.

*

That autumn, I went for a walk with Charlie around Morden Hall Park, freshly fallen leaves crunching under our feet as we trailed through the fields and gardens. He told me about his plans at Christmas to visit his girlfriend's family in Canada – he'd settled down since our dinner-party days. I told him about a dating app date I'd been on that turned out to be with a friend of his from uni. The man in question was nice, but I decided he wasn't for me.

Later, we went for a curry, and I joked to Charlie that my track record with his friends hadn't exactly been successful.

'Are you referring to Dan?' he said.

'Yes,' I replied. 'It was quite strange, we went on a date earlier this year while you were on holiday, and then I just never heard from him. I don't know if he even told you about it.'

He looked at me. I could tell he wasn't quite sure what to say. 'He told me he messaged you over the summer and you kind of shut it down.'

'Well, yeah, it was a bit late by then.'

Again, Charlie avoided my eyes, and then he said, 'The thing is, you guys are attracted to each other, and so I think anytime you're both not seeing anyone, you're just going to naturally float towards each other. But I don't think it's anything more than that. I had that with someone from home too, so I get it. But my advice is to put a stop to it.'

I considered what he said, but I didn't think it was true. I'd thought there was potential for something more – why would I still be asking this question five years later? I changed the topic. They still lived together, and I didn't know quite how to articulate what I wanted to say. Even if I did, I should probably have been saying it to Dan instead of Charlie.

In December, Dan slid into my DMs – the technique definitely had a name by now – to tell me a few local friends were going to the pub on Christmas Eve and I was welcome to join.

My mum gave me a lift. In the car, she turned to me and asked: 'Are you maybe going to kiss Dan Smith tonight?'

'No, Mother. I'm done with that.'

She gave me a look that implied she didn't believe me.

(My mum loves knowing the details of my love life and, in general, I do tell her what's been going on. She also never misses an opportunity to set me up, especially as I have got older. One time we were on the tube and I changed seats when someone got off to be closer to her. The man I was now sitting beside looked at me and then at her, trying to figure out why I had moved, and she said, in a coy voice, 'I don't know her. She's moved to sit closer to a cute man like you.' He laughed, I laughed. He actually was quite cute. And so I didn't mind. In fact, I rarely do, because she always does it in a silly way. She's not like some overbearing mums in romcoms. She'd never fix me up with hideous people for the sake of it; she has never insulted me or put the fact I'm single down to my job.)

Inside the pub, it was packed. Dan was in a room at the back with twenty or so friends, many of whom I hadn't seen in years. My cheeks quickly went rosy as we hopped between the court-yard for the smokers and the warm confines of the pub. James, another other old friend from school, had also received a last-minute invite, but he arrived late because he'd been having dinner with his family.

The owner of the pub is a local guy who was a few years above us at school, so he agreed to do a lock-in for a few extra hours. Time still slipped away, though, and soon he was booting us out. That's the funny thing about going home for Christmas as an adult; you end up reverting to adolescent patterns. We went round the group, asking who might have a free house, who could continue the party? But it was Christmas Eve – technically Christmas Day, as it was after midnight – so no one volunteered.

I suggested we go back to mine. My mum runs a bed and breakfast, and there's a flat above the garage that is effectively soundproof. I thought I knew where the key was, but I wasn't totally sure. It was a risk; it would take us twenty minutes to walk there, and then everyone would have to turn around if I couldn't find the key.

At the sound of this, most people decided it was time for bed. Two people didn't, though. Dan Smith. And James.

We walked along the country lane in the dark, the sea of stars above us providing just the right amount of light. We chatted away, but I wasn't really listening; my mind was fizzing. I had told myself I would not kiss Dan Smith again, and suddenly it was looking more than likely. But what about James?

I disappeared into the house to look for the key and some extra alcohol. The boys waited outside.

A few minutes later, I poked my head around the door and revealed the key. We were in.

The flat has an open-plan bedroom/sitting area, so Dan and I plopped down on the bed and James pulled up an armchair opposite. We drank most of a bottle of gin and an entire set of Fever Tree tangerine tonics that had been earmarked for Christmas Day cocktails, unbeknown to me (sorry, Mum – again).

The conversation quickly turned to dating: all three of us talked about the people we'd liked and the ones we hadn't, our most ridiculous reasons for ending something with someone, the icks we couldn't explain, the people who had captured our hearts and then broken them in two.

At one point, Dan said, 'Well, actually, Lizzie and I have been on a few dates.'

My mouth dropped open. 'Um, one. We've been on one.'

James looked perplexed. 'What? You two? When?'

'We went on ONE, earlier this year,' I said.

Dan jumped in. 'Oh, but there's been a few others too.'

'What others?' I said. 'You can't count the house parties from five years ago where we ended up sleeping together as *dates*.' I was laughing, but also telling him off.

'I think I can.' He was playing with me too.

James decided at that moment to go outside for a cigarette. When he did, Dan leaned in and gave me a tipsy, lingering, lovely kiss. It was indeed one of the better kisses of my life. There was something about the moment that felt just right.

We heard the door swing open and we pulled apart, eyes still locked. Then James was there, and we were out of the moment.

James told us about his exploration of heavy techno kink clubs, particularly in Berlin. We acknowledged the fact that because there were three of us and we were all single, some people might assume the night would go one way.

'I've done that before, and I'm not planning on doing it with you two,' I shared.

James went one further: 'Don't worry, Lizzie, you're not my type.'

I was mildly insulted by this, and asked him why. He said I was blonde and fair, and he went for darker brunettes.

I said, 'Fine.'

James, on the other hand, is very much my type. Or really, most people's type. Tall, dark and handsome. The next day, when I mentioned he'd been at the pub to my sister, her instant reaction was, 'Oh my god, stop. I always thought he was hot on the school bus.'

At some ridiculous hour – 4am? 5am? – we all stretched out on the bed, closing our eyes as we fell asleep, but still softly nattering.

Now, the next part of this story is not one that I am particularly proud of. It's one of the reasons why Dan Smith and I became so messy.

Because what happened next was that James leaned in and kissed me. And it was nice. And unlike with Dan, there was no fear of falling back into an old pattern. And so we kissed again.

'Is Dan asleep?' I whispered.

'Yes, he is. I wouldn't have kissed you otherwise.'

We kept kissing. All the while, Dan lay next to us, sound asleep.

Together, James and I got up and went into what I can only

describe as a rather large cupboard. Our clothes were flying off. James grabbed a towel and laid it on the floor.

'What are you doing?' I asked.

'Making it more comfortable,' he whispered back.

We were laughing that specific kind of laughter where you're trying to be quiet and you're totally not succeeding. In the next room, we heard Dan roll over and let out a big snore. We froze until we were sure he hadn't woken up.

'We need to get out of here; it's too weird,' I said.

'But where will we go?' James replied.

'I have a bedroom in the house with an actual bed, believe it or not,' I told him.

We crept out of the flat and into the house, and spent the early hours of Christmas morning enjoying each other's natural gifts. James has many. I won't bore you by listing them all, but know I was impressed with his package. Sorry. I can't help myself. He told me he hadn't been working out because of an injury; I really didn't notice, or care.

At one point, I asked him teasingly, 'So I'm still not your type, am I?'

'You don't have to be my type for me to fancy you.' He smirked.

The sleep was minimal, and when I woke with a start, I suddenly panicked about my mum going to grab something from the flat and finding Dan there in god knows what state. I texted her.

> Got home safe! By the way Dan Smith is in the flat. Happy Christmas! Stockings at 9?

I hoped I could distract her by casually sandwiching it in the message.

She replied:

> No running water in flat. Why didn't he stay in the house?

Shortly afterwards, she knocked on my door for a millisecond before opening it.

I shrieked, 'Wait, sorry, Mum, there's someone in here.'

'Dan Smith?' she asked.

'No, Mum, it's – it's someone else. Sorry, we'll come out in a min.'

Safe to say, my mum was confused.

I turned to James. 'Will you come up to the flat with me? Check if Dan is there?'

'Of course,' he replied. 'And maybe let's not mention what happened between us. I just feel a bit weird about it with the history,' I said.

'I don't think you need to feel weird – but yeah, I don't mind.'

We went up to the flat, but I wasn't expecting Dan to still be there. Surely he would have woken up, not known where we had gone, and decided it was time to head home. His parents would be looking for him. James's had already called him three times to figure out why he wasn't at the breakfast table.

But when we knocked on the door, he opened it with a flourish.

'Hello! By the way, the toilet isn't working because there's no water in the flat,' I blurted. But I was too late.

'Yes, I already found that out,' he said.

'Oh, does that mean . . .?'

'I've tried various techniques and I think the evidence is gone now.'

'How?' I asked.

'Trust me, you do not want to know the details.'

We all laughed.

'Where did you guys go?' asked Dan.

'Um, it was cold in the flat, so we moved inside, but you were out for the count,' I replied.

The two boys set off down the driveway, but not before both my mum and stepdad had stepped into their path. They'd been watching from inside through the window like two nosy neighbours – except for the fact that this was, of course, their own house.

'Happy Christmas,' my mum said. 'Are you sure you don't want to stay for breakfast?'

'Which one of you is Dan Smith and which one is James?' my stepdad joined in.

Dan lurched forward and gave them both a big hug. 'Happy Christmas.'

James proffered his hand for a formal shake. 'Yes, happy Christmas. Thank you, I have heard legends of your pancakes, but we really must go home before my parents kill me.'

I spent most of the day feeling quite hungover, and had to slink off at one point for a nap. My mum very much enjoyed making various jokes about what I'd been up to.

'James is very handsome. Thanks for bringing wine and sauciness to the day,' she said, with a twinkle in her eye.

James and I messaged on and off for a bit, but it was obvious this was a one-off; there wasn't any depth to our connection. Then Dan messaged a few days later, and it was flirty. I didn't know at the time whether he had any idea about what had happened with James. Perhaps James had told Dan on the walk home? They were friends, after all. Maybe that was why Dan was messaging me again. He had a habit of becoming more interested whenever I was less available.

Or maybe he didn't know, and he just thought it was romantic we'd kissed on Christmas Eve. It was cuffing season, after all, so perhaps he wanted to see where it might lead. Or maybe it just wasn't that deep. Maybe he'd kissed me, and he was feeling lonely during Twixmas, and he wanted to have sex.

On New Year's Eve, we exchanged a series of voice notes. I was at a small party with my housemate Dhara and my good friend Nick, and together we drunkenly dissected whether it was a good idea for me to fall back into something with Dan.

'I mean, this hasn't worked multiple times before, right?' Nick said.

'Shhh, Nick.'

'I'm team James,' said Dhara as she poked out her tongue.

'Right I'm going to voice-note him now. Nick, if you could just continue talking so it appears as if I'm surrounded by eligible young men.' I was half joking, half not. Nick took the brief too far and shouted something about being ready to come while I was mid-voice note. It sent. I listened to it back and decided it was garbled enough to be okay.

I may not have had a midnight kiss that year, but hearing Dan Smith's voice as we entered 2023 made my heart flutter: the message was sweeter than usual, telling me he had high hopes for the year ahead for me, and that he was already looking forward to my birthday celebrations. No doubt the number of shots he had inhaled that night had played a part in this.

A few weeks later he invited me to a dinner party at his house. There were six of us again, although no Charlie, as he was away with his girlfriend. Dan cooked us a Chinese feast using his new air-fryer, which he waxed lyrical about, and then we ribbed him for turning thirty before the rest of us and instantly becoming excited about air-fryers. Someone had brought a bottle of coffee-flavoured tequila, and we all drank far too much.

I told him about the idea for this book. At the time, it was just a seed of an idea – something I had wanted to do for a long time, but was only just feeling brave enough to share with the world.

'I think it will be great,' he said.

'Do you think you'll come across well?' I asked him.

'Of course,' he said.

'Why do you think that?'

'Because I'm the one you'll end up with at the end.'

I guffawed; it was so bold and so ridiculous, and still I loved that he had said it. 'That would involve us actually going on several dates, though,' I said. 'Last time we tried that, you just never messaged me afterwards.'

'Neither did you,' he said.

'Yeah, but it was your turn to instigate,' I said.

'I didn't see it that way,' he replied.

At one point, Dan scooped me up and carried me with a flourish to his room. We kissed for a good twenty minutes and our clothes stayed on. It was wonderful and dramatic and hilarious all at once. We could hear the dinner party continuing in the other room, and we returned as if nothing had happened.

The others had, by this point, started to take various drugs, which meant that the atmosphere had changed. Within another thirty minutes, I was ready to sleep, but knew the party wouldn't be over for a few hours. I told Dan, 'I'm going to bed,' and he nodded but stayed with the others. He was the host, after all, but as time went on I grew annoyed he hadn't crawled in next to me.

That week, he left for a holiday in Costa Rica and I didn't hear much from him. I'd slept with him and he'd lost interest, again. I went on a ski trip, met an alluring and amusing French man, and promptly forgot about Dan.

Until, that is, my thirtieth birthday party, a month or so later.

Dan had missed another good pal's birthday to attend, and was by my side most of the night. He had a knack for knowing when I was going to give up on him, turning up at just the right moment. It's that commitment-phobe bat signal again. I never thought about cutting him out of my life, either; it hadn't been that serious and we had too many shared friends.

That night, I kept finding him in the smoking area, chatting to my mum and my dad's girlfriend, Lana. He was charming and flirty and generally lovely. He was the last one on the dance floor with just a few of my closest girlfriends. He came home with me and we slept on the sofa (I had a number of friends and my sister staying the night, so there wasn't a double bed free). We kissed, but there was no sex; I wasn't sure I wanted that with him again.

The next day my mum and stepdad arrived for a walk, and the first thing my mum did was walk around the living room, lifting up the sofa cushions and peering behind blinds.

'What are you doing?' I asked.

'Looking for Dan Smith,' my mum replied.

My friends all laughed. We discussed the boy at length, and how we'd been hot and cold for so long.

'You just need to get him out of your system,' my mum said.

'What do you meaaaan?' I was sprawled on the sofa.

'I don't think he's the one, but I think until you just properly date him, you won't know. He'll remain this "maybe" forever. Just go on as many dates with him as you can, and then leave it be. Or not. But then you'll know.'

I considered her theory, turning it over and over in my mind.

'It's so obvious he is infatuated with you,' Hannah said. 'He followed you around like a puppy dog all night.'

My friend Emily, who had travelled to the party from Paris, chimed in. 'I think so too. Also, I think he just *gets* you. He knows exactly who you are, and that is exactly why he is obsessed with you. He kept talking about you last night.'

'If he's infatuated with me, then why doesn't he ask me out?!'

'I think he's intimidated,' said Dhara. 'You just wrote an article about how you fell for another boy on a ski holiday.'

'I think that's why he's interested again,' I said. 'He always creeps back when he feels like I'm about to be out of reach.'

'I don't like him,' my sister said. 'He essentially ghosted you last year.'

'He didn't ghost me,' I said. 'He just didn't message and neither did I.'

I decided my mum was right. I just needed to push forward with Dan Smith and go on enough dates so we could figure out if we did mean anything to each other. I needed to stop playing games and see once and for all. Were we meant to be, or were we just a halfway house for each other? This limbo land wasn't doing either of us any favours. I didn't want him to be a question mark, the one that got away. I wanted him to either be something, or nothing.

A week later, we were on a date. First some drinks in a pub, and then fried chicken and beers in Covent Garden. I told him about James and Christmas Eve, as I didn't want it to come out later and for it to feel like I was hiding something. At first, he laughed and thought I was winding him up.

I persisted, 'No I'm not joking. In a strange way, I think it happened because I was trying so hard not to get with you. Because that never ends up leading anywhere.'

He was shocked and definitely hadn't known. It was incredibly awkward. The conversation continued, but I could tell his mind was somewhere else, processing what I'd said. I thought perhaps it was over before it had even started. And then it was fine, and we never spoke of it again.

Over the next three months, we saw each other most weekends; sometimes there'd be a gap of a week or so in between. We didn't text much, but I told myself that was because he wasn't a texter. Sometimes the sex was good, but it was never excellent. I told myself it meant I really liked him, because I was willing to look past our occasional incompatibility.

My housemate Dhara was also seeing an intermittent texter at that time: someone who would wave big green flags of interest one day (hello, suggesting and booking to do a half-marathon together), and then nothing. Indeed, instead of the green flags, there would be only red ones. I had the same thing with Dan Smith.

It meant that Dhara and I often goaded each other into sending the boys a message, asking them to do something when it had been too long since they'd last suggested a date and then helping each other endure the intervening hours before they replied. There was one particularly bleak Saturday morning when we were both sitting on the sofa, our phones on the coffee table in front of us, just the right distance away to pretend that we weren't waiting on a message, but also close enough that we would see immediately if the screen lit up. Two women, two phones, two thousand volts of anxious energy in the room.

'Maybe we should just try screaming into the abyss?' I suggested to Dhara.

'What? Why would we do that?'

'I don't know. I just have so much nervous energy and I can feel you do too. Maybe that will make it disappear? Then we can move on with our day.'

'At this point, I'm willing to try anything.'

'Okay ... Three, two, one ...' We both screamed, and then crumpled with laughter. It was giving unhinged girlies, but it was fun to embrace how on edge we were rather than ignore it. Next time you're left on read, you might want to try it, preferably in sync with a good friend. In fact, it's become a core memory of my friendship with Dhara, because we were going through exactly the same thing and each knew exactly how the other felt.

It also reminded me of multiple scenes in *He's Just Not That Into You*, each of which depict lead single gal Gigi waiting by her phone for a call from a man. She comes up with a list of all the ridiculous reasons why each man might not have called: he's out of town on business, he lost her number, his grandmother died. She even convinces herself it would be a good idea to stage a run-in with one of her dates, so she turns up at a favourite haunt of his armed with a pen that he'd lost on their last date. It shows exactly how overthinking can become so dangerous, leading you to behave in strange ways. This scene has stayed with me because while it's veering on the ridiculous, we can all still relate. We've all come up with the convoluted reasons why they've not been in touch; we've all considered going to a party because there's a chance we might run into them. Or at least, my friends and I have. I once let a man leave my house without telling him he'd left his wallet on my dresser, thinking it would give us an excuse to see each other again sooner, thinking maybe he'd done it on purpose. I was young and dumb.

The important thing to remember is the actual text is never as bad as waiting for the text, because at least then you know what you're dealing with: if it's over, it's over. And wishing time away isn't just pointless; it's also a disservice to your life. Time is a privilege.

One other lesson Gigi taught me was that we should never be disappointed to read messages from our friends and family. Whenever the phone rings, she leaps to answer it – only to be frustrated to find it's her mother and not the future love of her life. Every time I watch this now, I feel so sad for her. She's too caught up in her dating world to make the most of the people around her who already love her.

And I know I've behaved like this too, hearing my phone buzz but feeling a twinge of disappointment that the WhatsApp isn't from the man I've been waiting to hear from, when really I should be celebrating the people who do care about me, who check in on me, who send me silly messages and heartfelt ones too. Sometimes it takes seeing your behaviour mirrored on screen to acknowledge how stupid it is.

When Dan Smith did reply – and he always did, though some-times after several days – we would take it in turns to plan the dates. We went to exhibitions, to Spanish plays, to nice restaur-ants, to arthouse films, to wine bars, to immersive experiences. He remembered things I'd mentioned in passing that I wanted to do, and planned dates around them. I enjoyed spending time with him but sometimes I wondered whether it was because of all the exciting things we were doing rather than his company. We never just went round to each other's places to spend time together. We never hung around the next day, drawing an evening out into a whole weekend. There was always an activity, an action plan. Something not just to do but to discuss.

One time, he gave me a card with a handwritten rhyming poem all about me; part of it was even in Spanish. Swoon. I thought it was so romantic that I told all my friends. When, a month or so later, he revealed it was written by ChatGPT, he didn't understand why it suddenly meant so much less to me.

Meanwhile, the alluring and amusing French man, Max, whom I'd met and fallen for on a ski trip a few months earlier (more on that later), was still hovering in a corner of my mind. He'd text me funny things, send me pictures of him on the platform at sea (he worked on an oil rig), and record silly voice notes. I did the same back, but as I continued to see Dan, it became more confusing. I knew I still liked Max, but it seemed inconceivable that it could work; we lived in different countries and he worked offshore. I felt like I had to pursue Dan first; there was more shared history and a more realistic future. It was time I found a nice sensible boyfriend instead of chasing wild men who worked on oil rigs. Or that's what I thought.

One day, Max spontaneously invited me to Berlin for the weekend. I wanted to go so badly, but I didn't. Things felt too far along with Dan, even though I still didn't know what we were.

Hannah told me I should go to Berlin: 'You haven't had the exclusive conversation, and I think you like Max more.'

'I would be so hurt if Dan told me he was doing the same in reverse, though. I need to give this a proper go to know once and for all.' So I turned down the fun weekend away with a boy who was doing everything Dan wasn't (communicating often, taking the initiative and making me feel wanted).

A few weeks later, Dan and I went on what turned out to be our last date. I spent the morning panicking that what I'd organised (a walk through north London) wasn't fun enough and the weather wouldn't be good enough. I booked last-minute tickets to something and breathed a sigh of relief. But soon even that gave me a niggling feeling in my stomach: if this many dates in, we couldn't just let each other be the main event, what did that mean? I knew deep down it wasn't a good thing. The show was impressive, but the evening that followed felt different from usual, as if, perhaps, there was something between us unsaid. The sky was grey and I felt grey. I had the overwhelming sense that someone had turned down the dial on our connection, and neither of us knew how to turn it back up.

In the morning, we left the house at the same time. He was running to work, so we said goodbye, and then I strolled down the street alone, watching him become a dot in the distance and then disappear into nothing at all. And in that moment, I knew: I wouldn't see Dan Smith again.

And still I persisted. There had been something there, so maybe the dial would readjust again and we'd find our rhythm. I held on to the idea of him, even when I knew that something wasn't right. I wanted to hear the click-clack of our puzzle pieces slotting together so desperately I was pushing and pounding them like a toddler who can't see the obvious mismatch. Of course, it's easier to say this now, with distance, but at the time I felt we had come so far that it had to work.

I had fallen victim to the sunk-cost fallacy – the idea that we've invested however many months or years of time in a person, so we want to see it through even if it no longer feels right. If, instead of a relationship, this had been a business, it's likely I would have been able to see that it was irrational to keep it going when it was losing money just because of the effort I'd put in. I could have forgotten the irrecoverable costs, and just analysed the future profits (or lack thereof). But this wasn't a business, it was emotional.

And so I continued to message Dan, even though I could feel him slipping away, and even though, by this point, I was unsure myself. The break between messages became longer and longer. I knew one thing for certain: I couldn't face another situation where we simply stopped talking. Maybe it would be less painful for both of us, but that would also leave the door open for the future, and I couldn't do that to myself.

I called him, and we had a strange sort of conversation that was almost normal.

And then I said, 'Look, the reason I'm calling is because I wanted to ask where your head is at. I know we haven't really talked about this, but I do like you, and I do want to keep seeing you – but I feel like something has changed for you.'

Because I did like him. I wasn't totally sure if we were meant to be something more, but I couldn't end it yet again with, 'It kind of works, it kind of doesn't.' I couldn't bear for the only closure to be, 'Maybe now isn't the right time, but maybe in two years, or ten, it will be.' I needed to know we had tried and decided it didn't work, and that we would never try again.

'Oh, um, sorry, is this because I haven't been texting as much?' he asked.

I was surprised that he hadn't been expecting my question. To me, it was obvious this was the one purpose of the call.

'I guess. I mean, you've never texted loads – but yeah, it does feel different.'

He waited and then said: 'Well, I found out my work is going to let me go on that sabbatical to South America I wanted to take next year, so I'm going to move home in a few months. And I guess I just started counting down the days, and I know how busy we both are, and I realised it just wasn't going to work from then.'

I took a moment. 'Okay. When were you planning on telling me this?'

'Sorry. I only just found out.' A pause. 'And I thought we were just casually dating. We would just decide during the week when we were seeing each other – it's not like we were planning far in advance. And we didn't text that much.'

His words pierced through me. He was diminishing what had been between us to make it seem like less of a big deal. His goal may have been to make me feel less sad, but it made me feel worse. It was belittling.

'I'm sorry, that's not what I thought we were doing. I thought we were dating each other to see if we could be anything more. It felt different to before.'

A younger version of me might have just agreed, said, 'No worries,' and put down the phone, but the older I get the less scared I am. The more honest I can be. And if it was ending anyway, what was the point of saving face? I have no doubt that crying and vulnerability can be superpowers. We shouldn't be ashamed of showing how we really feel; we should celebrate open emotions.

He backtracked quickly, 'No, you're right. I guess that was what we were doing.'

A long silence. A silence that told me we had our answer to whether we could be anything more.

But it was an amicable end – or as amicable as ends can be.

Dan Smith came to the realisation sooner than I had that we were better as friends, even if he hadn't been brave enough to tell me without being pushed. That was why things ended, not because he had a sabbatical coming up. I only wish he'd had the guts to tell me the truth straight, as that is ultimately far kinder than a white lie that slowly unravels. And his did.

We didn't speak after it ended, as I specifically asked him not to message me. I knew I needed the space, and I surprised myself by getting over him quicker than expected. It showed me how I really felt.

Looking back, I know I would have eventually reached the same conclusion as Dan, but likewise I hadn't been brave enough to call it a day when I should have. I wanted it to work, but sometimes, that isn't enough. Sometimes, it's not the right thing for your heart. And if they are just not that into you, it will never be enough. And that works both ways. Waiting for texts can create a nervous energy that might feel like butterflies, but with distance you are able to see that it's not.

The next time we saw each other was on Christmas Eve at the annual trip to the pub. Worried that it might be awkward, that it might make me feel strange, I nearly didn't go. At the last minute, I decided I wouldn't let one old flame prevent me from a fun evening with friends. And the magic thing was that I didn't feel sad at all, even when I found out that he was still living in London and his excuses had been just that: excuses. He left early – whether or not that was because of me, I don't know.

At around 10pm, my mum and stepdad strolled into the pub. I hadn't been expecting them.

'What's going on?' I asked.

'Oh, nothing, we were just bored at home and thought this would be much more fun,' my mum replied.

I was glad Dan had already left, or my mum might have had a few words to say to him. And I'm not sure how that would have gone down.

James was still there, though, and my mum made a beeline for him. She had always preferred him since meeting him the previous year, asking again and again, 'But what about James? He's much more gorgeous. And he seems nice.'

'James, I've got those Fever Tree tangerine tonics in that I know you like, if you end up back at ours again later.' She squeezed his arm and winked. He tipped his head back laughing, and smiled at me from across the room.

My mum had been right about Dan: we had needed to see it through to close the door once and for all. Finally, we were ready to do that. I'm not sure we can go back in time to being just friends yet, as it would be tricky with the history. But maybe one day we will. And I'd be happy with that.

I didn't bring back any boys from school that year, and my mum and stepdad ended up being the ones with a stonking hangover on Christmas Day. It felt good to tease them about it, when they had done the same to me the year previously. It was payback time.

'Mum, maybe lay off the Jägerbombs next Christmas Eve,' I joked.

'What do you mean?' she asked.

'I saw you doing them at the bar, trying to get everyone to join in,' I said.

'Well, there isn't any alcohol in them, it's just Red Bull. It's supposed to prevent a hangover, not cause one,' she said confidently.

'Oh, Mum.' I laughed. Maybe I could actually teach her a few things in return.

Some things I've learned about friendship

♥ There is no faster way to bond with someone new than talking about your biggest heartbreaks.

♥ Picking up the phone is one of the truest acts of love.

♥ Close friends will carry you through the lowest of lows.

♥ And champion you through the highest of highs.

♥ They'll do things like bringing a Rolodex of men to lunch when you're heartbroken, or pretending to be a couples' therapist to help you with a crazy plan.

♥ Your friends are also the best speechwriters when it comes to tricky texts.

♥ Try to listen to your friends' advice, even if you aren't ready to follow it.

♥ *Hitch* is right. A woman's best friend must sign off on all big relationship decisions.

♥ Remind your friends why you love them often:

  • Like the fact they'll swap clothes with you on a random Tuesday so you can go home to a boy's and still have fresh work clothes.

  • Like the fact they always have the silliest stories.

  • Like the fact they are so passionate about knitting.

  • Like the fact they will say they want an early night and then be the last one on the dance floor. Every. Single. Time.

  • Like the fact they look at the menu online beforehand and know exactly what you should both order.

  • Like the fact they will watch multiple Jennifer Lopez romcoms in a row with you.

  • Like the fact they will always be there.

9

10 WAYS I FEEL LUKEWARM ABOUT YOU

Starring the one I didn't want to commit to

It's always been interesting to me how quickly you can forget the relationships and dates that you put an end to, yet when the other person decides it's over, the memories seem to glue themselves into your mind.

I've bought into the narrative before of thinking that I've constantly been dumped or not chosen, and that it's never the other way around. But that is simply not true. There are plenty of times when I have been the one to call it quits. The problem is that I don't bother to remember them, because they didn't mean as much to me. My friends often have to remind me of this, and in turn, I have had to do the same for them. I'm sure it's the same for the many romcom heroines who are portrayed as 'unlucky in love'; it's just that the filmmakers never focus on the men they *weren't* interested in. We might get one silly bad date story, but that's about it.

In my case, there was the man with whom I quickly realised I had nothing in common, and, as we sat on a park bench together, I assumed he must have also got the vibe that we were never going to see each other again. Instead, he turned to me and asked, 'So, do you kiss on a first date? You look like you would be a good kisser.' I physically flinched.

There was the man I dated for an entire summer, going for picnics in the park, and to comedy shows and dinners and drinks. He was kind, but I didn't really connect with him. He had just bought a flat and kept asking me to help with the interior design and come to Homebase with him, but I just wasn't invested. He took me to a casino and lost hundreds of pounds, and thought I would be impressed that he was so flippant with money.

There was the man who was a friend of a friend, who kept staring at my boobs when he thought I wouldn't notice. Who would say 'yum' every time he looked at me.

There was the man that I fancied so much that after our first date, I skipped all the way home. Another time, he cooked me dinner, and even made mini chocolate soufflés. But the more time we spent together, the more I realised we had different world views about too many important things, and so I couldn't see it ever working. The fact he had to order chips with every meal is beside the point.

There was the man who was an animator and a huge football fan. I was attracted to him, but didn't feel a deeper spark, so I turned it into a 'friends with benefits' scenario. He had his own flat, where we could watch Netflix and then have sex wherever we wanted.

There was the man I met for a date in a pub, and our conversation was so impressively boring I returned home before my housemates had even finished the episode of *Friends* they'd started as I left.

There was the man on the double date Hannah forced me to go on while we visited her family in Yorkshire. He got ID'd in the pub because he looked about twelve and was very awkward. I had to play pool with him for hours while Hannah canoodled with his friend. Hannah, you still owe me for that one.

And if I look through the 'Hidden' section of my Hinge, Bumble or the numerous other dating apps I've tried – aka the graveyard where bad or boring dates go to die – I can see that there have been many others. Men with whom, after one date or two, maybe a kiss, maybe something more, I've decided it wasn't meant to be.

Another reminder is the screenshots of hideous opening lines and bios that never led to a date but have provided endless amusement for me and my friends in our ridiculously named WhatsApp groups – 'Lunchtime smut' has some real gems.

'Always smell good, because the first hole you're going to penetrate is her nostrils.' Eeek.

'If you get down on two knees before I get down on one knee, then we will delete the app. Ladies first right ;).' Dear god, how do these kinds of men get any woman to go out with them?!

Now, that wasn't the case with Jack. I met him in my first week of university. I did like him, and I definitely haven't forgotten him. There were several times after we ended things that I even wondered, *What if?* I questioned whether it was just a case of bad timing, or whether I had been silly to be dismissive of him. But I didn't want a relationship at that time, and he did. And so the way I remember our story isn't quite the same as the others I've shared in this book. I don't remember as many of the details. I have to crawl further into the corners of my mind to piece everything together. Even then, there are just a few key moments; the rest is blurred.

I can see Jack sitting on the grass in a circle of freshers in the courtyard of our hall at university on the first day I met him. It was sunny and he had a lovely head of ginger hair (the type you want to run your fingers through) and a distinctive nasal laugh that was more like a chortle. It was cute; he would tilt his head back each time, his whole body vibrating. We spoke across the circle and I found out he was indie (the thrifted shirt was the first clue; the house music obsession the second), a good listener, and funny. I liked him immediately.

I can see the conversation that unfolded the following week with one of my new friends who would go on to be a lifelong one, becoming my housemate in at least three different cities.

Jess's eyes sparkled as she told me, 'I have a secret.'

'Go on,' I replied.

'Jack likes you!' she blurted out.

We were in the main building on campus, queuing for a panini. 'What? Oh, that's awkward. I don't like him.'

'You don't? I thought I could sense you flirting back,' she said.

'Wait, which Jack? The one with dark hair in our Spanish class?'

'No, the ginger one in our halls, you doofus!' she said. We had only known each other for a week at this point, but already she was playful with me. This is her sense of humour, and it's only become more sarcastic and more mocking in the decade or so we've been friends. In Jess's language, 'You're a total loser,' means 'I love you so much.' Or at least that's what I tell myself.

'Ohhhh. Interesting. Yes, I do like him.'

We laughed together. My mind had gone to the other Jack initally as we had seen him just before.

After that, knowing that Jack liked me made it easier to be more confident and forward around him. He was the same: I'm pretty sure Jess delivered the message back that I was interested too. I'm sure she had the same sparkle in her eye when she told him. We formed a group of ten or so, half girls and half boys, and Jack and I were both part of it. Together we would go on nights out to listen to trendy DJs – everyone had cooler taste in music than me – and we'd all sit on long tables in the hall at dinner.

But Jack and I also started spending lots of time together on our own. We'd message on Facebook or text and invite each other round. I'd go to his room in another building in our halls, and he would come to mine. We would watch films, and have mischievous, whimsical conversations late into the night. And we would fool around, too, but I wasn't ready for us to have sex.

Our love language was to tease each other. He would say things like, 'Elizabeth, your face is boring' or, 'Elizabeth, your face looks like Abraham Lincoln.' I would say something equally bizarre back: 'You remind me of an old and beardy garden gnome.' Maybe these insults were influenced by the trope that hating someone means you secretly fancy the pants off them.

Despite how much I liked him, though, I was adamant that I didn't want something serious. I wanted to keep spending time with him, sure, but I didn't want to be a girlfriend again just yet. It felt different to be on the other side: to be the emotionally unavailable one.

The reason I didn't want a relationship with Jack was, of course, nothing to do with him. It was all to do with another man. I wasn't completely over my first boyfriend, Ezra, despite having been the one to end it, and I also knew I had broken up with him in order to be on my own. So I couldn't just waltz into another relationship a couple of weeks later. I wanted to figure out who I was without a partner. I'd spent the last few years picking up hobbies and interests that were important to Ezra, and I wasn't sure if they were really mine. I needed to figure out who I was and who I wanted to be, without someone by my side.

I also knew it would be a while before I was comfortable having sex again. I'd waited a year with Ezra, and I couldn't just do it two weeks in with someone else. I told Jack this, and his expression was one of bewilderment: he couldn't believe how long I'd waited the first time. He didn't seem quite as understanding as I had hoped. He wasn't pressuring me, but he also wasn't reassuring me.

I remember the day that Jack left a deep green vintage jumper with Eeyore emblazoned across the front in my room. I thought it looked cute over leggings, and so I wore it down to the dinner hall. I thought Jack would catch a glimpse of me, do a double-take and then smile. Instead, he was angry. He came over and said, 'Lizzie, you can't act like my girlfriend *and* say you don't want to be my girlfriend.'

I pulled off the jumper sheepishly and handed it back to him. I felt like a twerp. How had I become the one that was messing the other person around?

Things came to an end after he returned home for a week and spent time with his parents. He had told them about us, about me, and they told him not to continue seeing me if I didn't want anything more. I knew exactly why they had told him that; I would have offered the same advice in their shoes. Still, I was sad, though not enough to change my mind. This made it far easier to move on, even when I hadn't got the ick yet.

We succeeded at staying friends – we had to, really, we were part of the same group – though there was an energy between us whenever we were both single for the next year or so that never really went away. When he did get a girlfriend – and he had a few – I can remember feeling a little jealous. I didn't want a relationship with him, but I also didn't want him to be with anyone else. It made no sense in actual terms, and yet it made total sense in my head.

Many years later, I bumped into Jack at an autumn wedding in a cosy barn. At one point, another friend introduced us.

'Oh, Lizzie, have you met Jack?'

'Yes, we've met.' I smiled.

'Yes, I think we have,' Jack replied.

It was like peering into the past and looking into the future at the same time: an alternative life that never was. I could see we would never have been right for each other in the long run; that we were always better as friends.

Some things I've learned about icks

💜 You can try to bury the ick, but it will always resurface – in an even stranger way.

💜 The first ick is thus a sign of the beginning of the end.

💜 Don't fight it – you will not escape it.

💜 The list of icks is unpredictable, irrational, ever growing and ever changing.

- Maybe it's seeing them use an extra-long hot-water bottle at night.

- Maybe it's because they constantly comment on a certain celebrity's Instagram as if they are friends.

- Maybe it's watching them clap when the airplane lands.

- Maybe it's that they refer to their mother as 'Mummy'.

- Maybe it's knowing they keep their toothbrush in the shower to save time.

- Maybe it's that they still use Lynx Africa.

- Maybe it's their long fingernails.

- Maybe it's the way they ran for the tube.

- Maybe it's that they don't wash their towel because, 'I'm always clean when I use it.'

- Explaining an ick can make you sound unempathetic, unkind and rude, but an ick is merely a symbol of something more.

- An ick is a message from your gut: a get-out card that shows how you're feeling without getting too deep.

- If you really liked them, that same thing that's giving you the ick might one day be one of the reasons you love them. But in this case, it's not.

- And once it's not, it never will be.

10

AMOUR ACTUALLY

Starring the one from the ski trip

I'm sure by now you can see that I'm a romantic through and through. I'd rather meet someone reaching for the same book in a cosy local bookshop than from a half-hearted swipe on my phone while binge-watching *Sex and the City*. Okay maybe I need to be a bit more realistic and a little less romcom and trade the bookshop for a bar, but you get the picture.

Yes, I've used the apps on and off, and yes, I've met people who've gone on to mean a lot to me. But the thing that is so off-putting about dating online is that it begins to feel like homework, where your mark doesn't seem to reflect the effort you put in. How many times, though, can you craft a witty response before the conversation just dies and you have to pick yourself up and try again? Or how many times can you message someone for hours only to realise you have zero mutual attraction in person? Talk to anyone on the dating-app scene, and I guarantee one of the words they will use to describe it is 'exhausting'.

Meeting someone in real life feels more exciting – and more like the start of a film-worthy love story – but it's also ... So. Much. Simpler.

And in my opinion, there is no better way to meet a potential flame in real life than on holiday. The only small snag, of course, is that it's unlikely they'll live near you. But hey, if you won't move for love, then you can't call yourself a true romantic, can you?

As it turns out, there's a particular category of holiday that's best for falling for someone: the skiing trip. There's something about the outdoorsy energy, the fact you can get to know each other over a whole week, and, of course, the copious amounts of Aperol at the après that forms the perfect equation. This is something so many friends and readers of my articles had told me over the years, but it took me until I was nearly thirty years old to find out for myself, when I flew to the Alps with one of my closest pals. I was hoping to channel my inner Bridget Jones, Jess her inner *Chalet Girl*. (Not the same Jess from university – this Jess is a friend from work. It turns out I have an affinity for wonderful Jessicas.)

Jess and I both fell numerous times on the slopes – and also for two particular men we met there.

Jess met her Danish fling early on, and I watched as their romance bloomed over the following days. I was happy for her, but decided I wouldn't be having my own ski romance. I wasn't going to force a connection where there wasn't one. There had been a few men who had caught my eye and seemed nice, but no one I was drawn to in particular.

Until Max. And then I was like a moth to a flame. We met in a crowded bar in Chamonix, and kissed almost immediately. It wasn't quite like the carefully curated TikTok videos where two quote-unquote strangers physically bump into each other on the street before promptly making out, but it wasn't far off.

There is even a photo we took shortly after meeting the French boys, a group of ten or so of us, with Max and I snogging front and centre. At the time I thought it was hilarious, verging on embarrassing, but now I look at it with great fondness. Partly because of what followed with Max, sure, but also because of how

I felt that night. Entirely out of my own head and caught up in the moment and the magic of meeting someone new.

It turned out we were all staying at the same hostel-like accommodation, the UCPA in Argentière outside Chamonix, but we somehow hadn't crossed paths until now. In between the kissing and dancing, I could see snippets of Max's personality which only made me fancy him more. He was fun and funny, sweet and silly. I only had a vague idea of who he was that night, but now that I've spent more time with him, I know for sure it wasn't just the tequila shots talking. That is to say, I would have been just as drawn to him in a bookshop as I was in that bar.

When people ask what my type is now, I know the answer: silly. It's the thing the men I have liked the most all have in common. It hasn't always been that way. I used to be drawn to serious deep-thinkers, but somewhere along the line something changed, and I'm glad it did. Find me a man who is funny in a quirky way, who says things that make you roll your eyes and laugh at the same time, who dances like a dad and isn't embarrassed by it – and I'm like putty.

Max is exactly like that. He's the one who will spin around the room at a party when no one else is dancing yet. He's the one who will pretend you are a giant rotisserie chicken in order to continue a joke from earlier in the evening. He's the one who will don a mock-eighteenth-century tunic for a night out just because he feels like it, and not care when strangers question why.

Over the rest of the week, we spent more time together, exchanging handwritten notes, chatting over Brie and Camembert after dinner, and walking hand in hand through the snow. We went to a local bar with live music and danced as if we knew each other far better. I was giddy with flirty feelings for him. When I saw him in the dining queue from afar, I would blush, my heart beating a little faster. We also made several visits to the yoga room on the top floor in the early hours (what did I say about there always being somewhere private in a hostel if you know where to look?).

This one even had a double mattress pushed up against the wall that we pulled into the centre of the space. It seemed too good to be true; I felt like Max had somehow arranged it.

We'd fall asleep unintentionally, naked and twisted together, and wake with a start – did we really want to find out if the chair pushed up against the door to prevent unknowing intruders would work? Reluctantly, we'd crawl back into our separate hostel beds.

In the final hours of our trip, as I packed my bags and had one last breakfast, I felt like a balloon the day after a party: unable to stop myself from slowly deflating, and feeling a little out of place. Max came over to say goodbye. We talked about visiting each other, but it felt like something you have to say rather than a proper invite. I'd been in this position before, so I knew what was coming. Maybe we'd message for a while, and then things would peter out and I'd wonder what could have been if we lived just a little closer. The balloon wouldn't burst; it would just diminish and diminish until there was only a limp, sad version of what had been left.

I should remind you that while Max is from Paris, he works offshore on an oil rig and so is often away for long periods of time. This wasn't that surprising to me – if anything, it fitted into the narrative of my dating life rather well. I've often joked with my friends that I can't fancy someone unless they live at least 5,000 miles away. So of course he couldn't just live in Paris; that wouldn't have been complicated enough.

However, Max surprised me.

After the trip, I had to tell him about an article I was writing. Whereas I had been up front with Evan that I was planning to write about him when I did my flat swap in New York, I hadn't told Max during the holiday. He'd known I was there for an article, but he thought it was about learning how to ski. You see, Jess and I had decided before we left that it would be weird to tell people we were there to see if it was easier to find romance on the slopes than back home on the apps. We were worried it might skew our results – either by putting people off, or maybe even the opposite. Neither of us wanted to find a beau who would do something grand just to see his name printed in a broadsheet. We really went into it hoping to find something real.

It was slightly awkward when, a week later, I admitted to Max that I might include a few details about our mini love affair. But he handled it well – or at least, he didn't tell me not to do it. He did know I'd written a couple of articles about my love life before, so it wasn't a total surprise. Jess's romantic interest wasn't quite as pleased, and insisted he was made anonymous. He thought Jess had tricked him, that she'd slept with him for the story rather than because she liked him. He couldn't have been more wrong. In fact, telling the boys about the article felt more like a romcom than any other part of the experience. There's always a bet or an article that gets revealed at the worst possible moment, meaning the couple risk losing each other, losing it all. Jess's man came around eventually when he saw she was exactly the girl he had met.

So there I was, sitting in the office, doing my day job, thinking I had it all under control – but I was about to encounter an unexpected obstacle. Out of the corner of my eye, I could see the picture editor marching over. She was smiling, but I knew it wasn't going to be good news for me. In front of all my colleagues she said, 'Lizzie, we need a picture of your fit French man.'

'Umm . . .' I could feel myself overheating. 'That's not going to be possible. I didn't ask him for one.'

'Well then, call him right now and ask him.' She was not backing down. She leaned on my desk as if she was going to wait right there while I spoke to him. Did she really think I was going to have that conversation at my desk?

'I mean, it's a little awkward to do that. Do I really have to? He's going to think I'm in love with him,' I said.

'I don't care how you do it, but please send it to me by the end of the day.' She walked off.

If this had been a Richard Curtis movie, I would probably have engaged in five minutes of posh swearing at this point: 'Fuck. Fuckity fuck.'

I tried to remain calm and opted for a message instead:

> Awkward question alert: the picture editor is asking if we can use a pic of you in the piece. Are you okay with this? I didn't include any originally but she is being very persistent.

The next ten minutes were horrible. I was sweating. I liked this man; I didn't want this to be the thing to put him off. My phone buzzed, I picked it up, and before I had time to read the message he had deleted it. Cue more panic. This was bad. This was embarrassing.

Finally, he replied. He wanted to know what the article would say before he gave his permission. I told him (not the exact words, but a summary) and he replied swiftly:

> That's awesome, thanks for sharing! I am comfortable sharing my face – and plus I trust you with it.

I stopped hyperventilating and breathed a deep sigh of relief.

> Okay, sorry – this is such a weird part of my life. I really appreciate it and I hope you like it when it comes out.

> Wouldn't have met otherwise, I guess.

My heart thumped and I felt giddy. I squished my face with my hands and let out an involuntary squeal. A squeal that said how much I liked him.

And then not only did he continue to message over the following weeks and then months, but he wanted to meet up. He suggested it a few times, sometimes with more material details than others – but the intention was there.

I was the problem. I had started seeing someone in London while he was working away (yes, Dan Smith, the halo-effect boy from school) and I felt like I was in limbo. I couldn't shut down the idea of Max, because I wasn't ready to say goodbye.

One time I remember reaching for my phone in a locker after a trampolining class, only to be greeted by a message from Max:

> Oh by the way, I am heading to Berlin this Saturday for a week or so. I'll be staying at my friends but if you wanna join, I'll be happy to share a place with you for a few days. I know it's a little last minute but who knows.

I was already flushed from the exercise, but somehow I managed to go a few shades pinker. The hair on my arms even stood up on end – I'm serious. My heart stopped for a moment then raced ahead. As you know, though, I didn't go.

I'm sure I came across as distant and at times perhaps disinterested. I never was; I just thought it was time to be sensible. I was thirty. I couldn't dismiss someone on my doorstep for someone else who would have been so much more complicated. I know now that was a mistake. You have to follow your heart. Even when it doesn't make much sense.

Max often laughed at me for putting too much meaning behind what others might see as simple coincidence. But the fact we ended up in the same corner of the world three times in eight months or so seems too storied to just be random. The first was, of course, our ski holiday in Chamonix, but then in the early summer we realised we would both be just outside Bordeaux over the same weekend. I was there for a wedding, and he was visiting

his grandmother and had a work party. By this point, I was defin-
itively single again.

We knew we would both be there, but hadn't ironed out the
details of where we would meet until the weekend itself. Perhaps
a lunch in Bordeaux before I flew? Or, I suggested, he could
come for dinner and stay the night at the Airbnb where I was
staying with a group of friends the night after the wedding. He
said he'd like to come, if I wanted him to. I hopped back and
forth with what I wanted; I had suggested it, but suddenly faced
with the reality, I panicked it might be awkward. He might
travel the hour or so to where I was only for us to discover that
the attraction that had existed in the snow-covered mountains
had melted long ago.

At one in the morning, I sent a series of tipsy messages, which
I then deleted before he could read them – and before I could
remember what I had said. I think maybe I was looking for reassurance, but he was fast asleep.

At 6am I woke up, filled with the anxiety that often comes
with a hangover. I wrote:

> Dear god, I am hungover … maybe it would be
> better to meet tomorrow instead.

I know now he was disappointed. A casual comment months
later revealed I'd hurt him by sending that message. I would have
felt the same. But he went along with what I said I wanted, and so
we met for lunch the next day instead.

It was nice. We spent a few hours together: we sat at an outside table in a sweet square for lunch, then took a stroll through
the city, followed by dessert somewhere else. We didn't kiss.
Something somehow was off, and I felt relieved he hadn't come
all the way to the Airbnb.

'I just found out I got a new job, and all being well, I've got two
months off in between,' I said.

'Oh really? Where do you think you'll go?' he asked.

'I'm not totally sure yet. Somewhere in Asia for a month – maybe Vietnam? Or India? Then the second month, I think I'll go to Bali. It's not far from Australia, so my sister will probably meet me there for a week or so.'

'Huh. I've got a big trip to Indonesia in September, actually.'

'What?' I said. 'You've got to be kidding.'

'No, really – with Gabriel, my friend you met in Chamonix. But I don't know how much time we'll spend in Bali; we want to go to the other islands. Java. Lombok. Yeah.'

'Oh yeah, I haven't looked into the other islands yet, but my friend recommended a few.'

I couldn't believe he'd once again planned a trip to the same place as me and at the same time. He reacted as if it was totally normal. Was this not the stars aligning?

We said goodbye and it felt like an anticlimax. Our holiday romance had been just that. My friend Charlie, who had done a ski season, had warned me that love at altitude rarely lasts in the real world. I thought that perhaps he was right.

We continued to message, but much less often than before; we both knew something had shifted, that perhaps what we had felt for each other no longer existed. So few holiday romances go the distance, but that's almost what makes them more special – like a supernova, they often burn bright and die young.

And so I didn't think about him when planning my trip away. Indonesia is a huge country; just because Max and I were both there at the same time, it didn't mean we would see each other. Maybe I would cross paths with Max, but maybe I wouldn't. At that point, I didn't mind either way.

Some things I've learned about dating apps

- ♥ A lot of men think they're six foot tall when they're not.

- ♥ Some people on there are purely in it to boost their own ego – the secret is spotting them fast.

- ♥ Don't leave it too long to meet.

- ♥ Don't meet up too quickly.

- ♥ *Love, Guaranteed* this is not. Sorry, made-for-Netflix romcom.

- ♥ People who seem lacklustre online rarely improve in person.

- ♥ If they've only got one pic and no bio they may be a serial killer. Or, at the very least, a catfish.

- ♥ The cheesier the chat-up line, the better the potential.

- ♥ I don't think the inventors fully thought through the addition of photos: how are you meant to unknowingly fall for your business nemesis à la *You've Got Mail*?

- ♥ There's too much choice.

- ♥ There's not enough choice.

- ♥ Meeting someone in real life will always feel so much more exciting.

11

EAT DANCE LOVE

Starring the one on the solo holiday

I'd like to say that thirty is just a number and I approached it in the same way I have other birthdays. But that would be a lie.

Why do we see this as such a significant age, particularly as women? Particularly as single women? Is it because it's the start of a new decade? Is it because it marks the end of our twenties? I'm sure it's both of these things, but it's also because of pop culture: the romcoms, songs and TV shows that remind us of society's expectations of what a thirty-year-old woman should and should not be.

There's a scene in *Friends* where Jennifer Aniston's Rachel Green turns thirty that I first watched when I was not much older than ten and have seen dozens of times since. I used to think it was funny because of how ridiculous it was. She is trying to comfort herself about not being where she thought she would be in life, but ends up going into full meltdown mode instead. The closer I got in age to Rachel, though, the less ridiculous she seemed to me – and the more I could see her panic mirrored in my own. I knew my single friends could relate to it too.

A clip of the scene started to do the rounds on social media. Don't tell me you haven't seen it. It goes something like this:

'Y'know what? I realised it was stupid to get upset about not having a husband and kids. All I really needed was a plan. See, I wanna have three kids … I should probably have the first of the three kids by the time I'm thirty-five, which gives me five years. I love this plan! I wanna marry this plan! So, if I wanna have my kids when I'm thirty-five I don't have to get pregnant until I'm thirty-four. Which gives Prada four years to start making maternity clothes. Oh, wait – but I do want to be married for a year before I get pregnant … No, so I don't have to get married until I'm thirty-three. That's three years, that's three whole years – oh, wait a minute though. I'll need a year and a half to plan the wedding, and I'd like to know the guy for a year, year and a half before we get engaged, which means I need to meet the guy by the time I'm … thirty.'

No pressure then, Rachel. For me, this scene captures so perfectly the anxiety that comes with a desire to have children and knowing that you have a biological clock. Not everyone wants to have kids, but I have always felt like I would. And that, quite frankly, was what was starting to fuck with my head.

Not to mention the horrible, misogynistic double standards that become apparent as we get older. Men get wrinkles and look distinguished; women get wrinkles and look haggard and need Botox. Men are handsome silver foxes and eligible bachelors; women who get left on the shelf turn into lonely spinsters with 300 cats. Men need to run their own Fortune 500 company to be happy; women need one of the big white weddings they've seen on screen (I think there is one in almost every romcom) to be happy. I don't believe any of this, but I've heard it on repeat so often that it's hard not to just scream at strangers in public to shut the hell up.

When I was twenty-eight, I was happy with being single. I knew I wanted to meet someone at some point, but I wasn't going to let that control how I felt about my life. As soon as I turned twenty-nine, though, there was a croaky little voice in my head that would whisper to me in quiet moments, 'You have twelve months left to find the one.' I tried to ignore it, but it was always there. Like some sort of evil witch in a fairy tale who was overly obsessed with my love life and my prospects of motherhood. So, like most evil witches in fairy tales then. And then it started getting louder and louder as the year went on. 'You have eleven months left to find the one.' Ten. Nine. Eight. This invisible countdown that no one else in my orbit was aware of said, 'If you have a kind and loving man by your side on the day you turn thirty, you'll be fine. If you don't, good luck.' Evil laugh optional.

I knew it was stupid, but I was struggling to find a way to stop the witchy voice in my head, even though I knew I didn't want my life to become a game of musical chairs, where whoever I was sitting on at the age of thirty would automatically be the one. I'd seen this happen to other people and knew it wasn't a fast-track to happiness. If anything, it was dangerous to think that way.

My friend Shreya felt similar to me: absolutely sure she wanted kids, and at the same time feeling like that possibility was slipping away. We no longer lived together, as she'd moved to another city for a job, but we would often have long phone calls from our bedrooms or as we each walked around a park.

On one of these calls, just four months or so before my own big birthday, Shreya told me, 'I've decided I'm going to be single on my thirtieth.'

'Oh, really?' I laughed.

'No, hear me out. I want to start this new decade on my own, knowing I don't need anyone else. If the right person comes along after that, great, but I don't want to fall into the trap of rushing to find someone just because of my age.'

Her words stuck with me and I kept thinking about them in the days that followed. I started to repeat them to myself like a mantra. And the more I said them, the better I felt. Technically nothing had changed, but I was reframing how I felt. Rewriting the script. And that small tweak changed everything. I couldn't hear the old voice anymore, because it was drowned out by the new one. And in that way, Shreya's wise words ended up being transformative for me (and her too). I wouldn't be sad about being single on my thirtieth birthday; it was just another day, and I was consciously choosing to be alone. I wasn't choosing to be alone forever, either, just for one day.

I decided the only feeling I should have on my thirtieth, and any future birthdays, was gratitude. That when it comes to analysing where I am in life, I should do everything to remember to be grateful for having lived another year, for having the chance to get older – no matter what that looks like. I may need to remember to reread this page in the year leading up to my fortieth.

Plus, while I could relate to Rachel Green spiralling about her age, I could see too that she was already living a life worth celebrating. The same goes for Carrie Bradshaw, Elizabeth Gilbert, Bridget Jones, Annie in *Bridesmaids* – the list goes on. If they didn't have it all figured out yet, then it was fine that I didn't either.

It worked. I spent the day with my family: my mum, my stepdad, my dad, my stepmum and my sister. That in itself, considering we live on three different continents and there was a time when my parents couldn't be in the same room, was magic. At the weekend, I had a party with close friends and family, drinking wine and eating cheese in a converted Victorian loo before enjoying some dancing and pizza. Not once did I wish there was a boyfriend in the background. As you'll remember from a few chapters ago, there was a man present (about whom you've already heard far too much), but when he tried to suggest he could be my date, I quickly shut him down. That night was my own. He couldn't take my moment away.

I had also realised that having children can look different to what you might have once expected, whether that means starting a family at a later age or an earlier age, through adoption or IVF, with someone you're not married to but plan to be with long-term, or with someone with whom you hadn't decided to spend more than a few months. It may even happen through the lens of being there for your friends' and family's children, which obviously isn't the same, but can also be powerful and positive. You can't ever really plan for a baby to happen just so, even when you're married or really want one. Once you understand that, you can see that there is no right time to meet the right person. There's just the right person.

What I have found funny are the rules my single friends have imposed on dating as they get older. One said she was not going to wear nice lingerie until it was an official relationship. Another said she was done spending money on men, so she refused to ever get an Uber back from her date's house – she would only get the bus. Funnily enough, both are now in relationships with these men – but I doubt it has anything to do with those specific rules.

Around six months after my thirtieth birthday, I interviewed for a travel editor role at *The Times* and saw my opportunity to have a break from London. I'd always wanted to go on a gap year, especially solo, but I had become attached to climbing the journalism career ladder, and I was afraid I would struggle to get back on if I just quit. My industry (like many others in the world of creatives) is one where you are constantly told that you are one of the 'lucky ones' and that, to echo *The Devil Wears Prada* catchphrase, 'a million girls would kill for your job'.

And so when I was offered the job, I knew this was my opportunity. I negotiated a start date two months after I had wrapped up at the *Telegraph* – it wasn't as long a break as I had dreamed of, but it meant I had the security of a job waiting when I got home and enough time for my own adventure.

As for the destination? That was easy. I did what any thirty-something woman seeking to find herself does, and plotted a trip to South East Asia. I chose just two destinations: Vietnam, for backpacking and *bánh mì*, and Bali, where I could live out my best *Eat Pray Love* life. I hadn't read the book, but I had grasped the general idea. In that time, I could also have squeezed in Cambodia, Laos and much more of Indonesia, as people continued to tell me, but as a travel writer, I often have just a few days in a place to crack the story. I wake up early and stay up late to see markets, culture and nature, to explore communities and to capture the buzz. I plan and I plan and I have tight itineraries. I've become an expert in capturing a feeling from the fleeting, but that means that the real luxury to me is to be able to linger.

And so that's exactly what I did. Other than the first hostel in Saigon and my flights to Vietnam and back from Indonesia, I didn't book a single thing ahead of my trip. And I did no research. I would rely on word of mouth, I decided. It felt liberating. (Okay, and a little scary for a type-A personality like me.)

A friend of mine, Emilie of the Shamrock crew, had gone travelling for a few months by herself earlier that year, and I messaged her in the days leading up to ask if she had any last-minute advice.

She said:

> First of all, you are going to have an AMAZING time. But know that there will be moments in that first week where you wonder why you went by yourself. The first few days I was in Cambodia, I was like, what the fuck have I done? But then I absolutely loved it. Just know that the doubt will pass and you'll feel so lucky to have got the chance to travel solo. Especially for such a long time.

It was the kindest thing she could have said. It meant that if (and when) I did question my decision to go alone, I would know I wasn't silly for feeling that way. There's a pressure when you go travelling to instantly have the best time and be comfortable on your own, right from the start, and that isn't always realistic.

Saigon

The first moment of doubt came on the long plane ride from London to Saigon. If you're anything like me, you'll get to your seat early and watch the procession of other passengers coming down the aisle, convinced that the person who will take the seat next to you will be indescribably hot and that you'll fall in love with them over the next twelve hours. Maybe you'll share a bag of pretzels; maybe you'll decide to watch the same film and start it at exactly the same time. Maybe you'll join the mile-high club. Could it be him? Or him? Oh, please let that gorgeous thirty-something man with short curly hair be sitting next to me. But no – it's a portly, older gentleman who smells of armpit sweat and tobacco, and keeps picking his nose.

Sadly, my airplane romance was not meant to be this time. Instead, I was sitting next to two women from South Korea who had been on a girls' trip to Paris, leaving their husbands and kids at home. They'd studied in the city in their early twenties, and described how amazing it felt to return together as if no time had passed.

When they asked where I was going and I told them about my two-month solo trip, they looked surprised. 'Alone? Are you not scared? Please be careful.'

I laughed nervously. 'Oh, I'll be fine.' I sounded more confident than I was.

When we landed, I said goodbye to them before heading down the aisle. As I made my way out of the airport, the humidity was off-the-charts high. I'd pre-booked a taxi to take me to the first hostel, knowing it would be late at night and I wouldn't have a Vietnamese SIM yet.

I'll start being a proper backpacker from tomorrow, I told myself.

The plan went smoothly, until the taxi dropped me off at the end of a long alleyway, with the driver gesturing that the car couldn't go any further. I looked around at the neon signs on either side of the alleyway, but saw none for the hostel. I had no map and knew a grand total of three Vietnamese words. But then there it was, and I breathed a sigh of relief.

I found my way upstairs to my dorm room and, as I was digging through my bags to find something cooler to slip on, a dreamy man in his thirties, whom I would later learn was called Raphael, walked in to grab his phone from a charger.

'Hi, did you just get here?' he asked.

'Yes, just got off a very long flight.'

'Where from?'

'London. Where are you from?'

'Bordeaux.'

Uh-oh. My personal danger zone.

'*Ah, t'es français.*'

'You speak French? Well, there's a few of us up on the rooftop if you want to join. We're singing karaoke – but don't let that put you off.'

'I'll see you up there. Just sorting out my bag.'

'See you.' He headed out of the room.

I looked in the mirror on the wall opposite and saw that I was smiling like an idiot. As if I'd formed a crush on the first person I met. You'll know by now I have a soft spot for French men. *Don't jump at the first man. You're here to be on your own*, I said to myself.

I avoided partaking in the karaoke – unaware that over the next month, this would become one of my main hobbies (not by choice) – drinking a beer instead with Raphael and a few others from England, Australia and Singapore.

We left around midnight to go to the 'walking street' (Saigon's version of Bangkok's Khao San Road), where men were breathing fire, women dressed like schoolgirls were dancing on podiums, and motorbikes were chugging past with fluffy dogs as passengers. We sat at a table on the street and ordered drinks, but not long afterwards the police arrived, and all the tables were cleared away before we fully realised what was going on. Then, when the police had passed, the tables reappeared and we sat down again as if the whole thing had never happened. It was a ritual that the staff of this illegal street vendor were clearly well versed in.

When we got back to the hostel, Raphael told me he was going to have one last drink on the rooftop. Did I want to join him? I did, but I was also exhausted, so I said I was going to bed. I thought to myself again, *You can't fall for someone on the first night. It hasn't even been twelve hours; please calm down.*

In the morning, I set off to explore on my own. Crossing the street proved to be my first hurdle. Saigon, or Ho Chi Minh as it is officially named (but no one actually calls it), is a city of motorbikes – some say there are as many as 7.3 million on the streets – and I spent longer than I should have on a corner, unsure when to step out into the traffic. It had been easy the night before with others leading the way, but now it was up to me. I'd already been told that if you waited for the bikes to stop, you would never be able to cross. The only rule to remember was not to lose your nerve and step backwards, because that was when you were most likely to end up in an accident.

I kept telling myself I would go in the next lull, and then I wouldn't, because that lull would never come. As Emilie had predicted, I had a moment of thinking, *What on earth made me decide I could do this on my own?* I couldn't even cross the bloody street. How was I going to get from one side of the country to the other?

But then an elderly Vietnamese man was at my side. He gave me a smile and a nod, and reached out his arm. I realised he wanted me to loop mine in his so he could lead me across the road. And so I folded my arm around his, and together we stepped out into traffic, walking across easily fifteen rows of motorbikes whizzing along. At the other side, he lifted his arm out of mine, nodded and went on his way. I could have cried. It was so simple and yet so kind. I shouted after him, 'Thank you, I mean ... *cảm ơn!*' – but he was already out of sight. Probably a good thing, as my pronunciation had been terrible to the point of incomprehensible. It was a reminder that sometimes you just have to keep going forwards, even when it feels impossible.

That would never have happened if I'd been holding hands with someone else, I thought.

In the afternoon, I decided to visit the War Remnants Museum. It was heartbreaking and horrifying and horrible to contemplate, especially given I'm half-American. Near the end of my visit, I exited one room and practically bumped into dreamy Raphael from the hostel. You know, the one I had already formed a crush on.

'Oh hello, Lizzie,' he said.

'Hi,' I replied.

'How long have you been here?'

'A couple hours, I'm nearly done.'

'You know this is where the exhibition begins, right? You start on the top floor and work your way down?'

'No, I didn't know that.' I laughed. 'I think I've done the whole thing in reverse, which, come to think of it, now makes sense.'

'What are you going to do after?'

'Might go for a drink. Do you want to join when you're done?'

'I would like to, but I'm actually going to the airport after this. Flying to Hội An for the next few days.'

I couldn't help but feel a little bit disappointed. I thought we would at least have another evening together before going our separate ways. When I had refused his offer of a nightcap, it was because I had counted on a second chance.

'Oh, that's a shame,' I said.

'It is. Let me know if you end up in Hội An before Thursday.'

I smiled. A younger version of me might have changed my plans to go sooner, but I wanted to spend more time in Saigon. I had, thankfully, by the grand old age of thirty learned to follow what I wanted to do, not morph myself to fit in with a boy I barely knew and his specific plans.

So, rather than hopping on a plane like a hopeless romantic – which I still proudly self-identify as, albeit with caveats – that evening I did what I most wanted to. Which was to go on a motorbike food tour with a local. In my case, with a university student in her twenties called Mai. Several friends had raved about the tours as the best way to see the city and eat the best food, too. It cost £30, cheaper than a lot of dinners in London, and I would get my own private guide.

Mai picked me up outside my hostel and taught me how to get on the back of the bike safely, avoiding the exhaust pipe. 'So many people get burns here; they call it the Saigon Kiss, or up north, the Hanoi tattoo,' she explained. It had been a long time since I had been on a motorbike, and I was a little nervous knowing how close you get to other bikes in the heavy traffic.

Mai took me out to districts five and six as the sun was setting, chatting over her shoulder as we went. Soon, we were sitting eating delicious *bánh phát*, little savoury pancakes topped with juicy prawns, with a huge plate of fresh herbs and sauces for dipping. We also went to a fabulous pho place, had *bánh mì* from a street-side stall, tried broken rice and much more. All the stops were far from the beaten tourist path, so much so that I didn't see another traveller for the six hours I was with Mai. The best bit, though, was getting to hear about her life – and, what a surprise, we bonded most by talking about our dating experiences. She told me matter-of-factly that she'd had lots of boyfriends, and the first detail she always told her mum about a new boyfriend was that they were from district four. The district had once been known for its gangsters, and it was a failsafe way to wind up her mum. She laughed just thinking about it.

Over the next week, I became very comfortable in the city that had been so foreign to me just a few days earlier. And I found myself with a new crush practically every day. There was the sweet and earthy Scottish man with an adventurous spirit who lived in Melbourne. I could listen to his voice for hours, his accent a meandering and melodic mix of his two homes. There was the gnarly west-coast Aussie, who loved the outdoors and photography and hardly ever wore shoes. I couldn't quite figure him out, and that made him all the more fascinating. There was the short Mexican guy who was too young for me, but the way his eyes lit up when he told a story was intoxicating. He fell asleep on my shoulder on a long bus ride after a day trip, and my heart swooned.

Why was it so easy to fancy people here compared to back in London, where crushes were few and far between? It was the same as the ski trip I had been on. Here, you met people in real life and got to know them exactly as they were. I'd deleted my dating apps for the trip away and never once craved them. This was just the first week, but the same was true two months later. Because instead of colouring in the details of a man that I may or may not meet via texts and memes and gifs, he was right there in front of me.

There was also no pressure for something to develop. And as a serial overthinker who can't help but wonder after a great first date what we might serve as the dessert at our dinner parties (a tarte tatin with one man; a pistachio baklava with another) or what kind of first home we'll get (a cottage with one; a campervan with another), this is a humongous help to me. Because then I don't get too caught up in thinking too far ahead and putting too much pressure on each moment; and because then I also don't write someone wonderful off for something trivial like the fact they wear a signet ring.

Plus, by staying in hostels, I was meeting new people every day and it was totally normal, if not encouraged, to say hello and strike up a conversation if you spotted another solo traveller out and about in a way that you just wouldn't in a café in London. And the travellers that were there, especially the ones choosing to holiday solo, were more often than not adventurous, and passionate, and confident. And those are three things I find very attractive.

Hội An

Soon I decided it was time for the next place, but I found it harder to leave than I had expected. I knew that as soon as I left, I would be on my own again. I'd settled into Saigon and found my people, as it were, but I was about to shake it all up and start over. I'd have to choose a new hostel, find new friends, and feel lost again in a new city.

But I found my girls quickly in the next stop of Hội An, thanks to another sociable hostel. Not a party place, but one that drew intriguing twenty- and thirty-somethings together around family-style meals and a suntrap of a pool. It was closer to the beach, meaning it felt really relaxed, but a quick Grab ride (aka Uber for motorbikes) past fabulous rice fields would drop you in the town's pretty centre.

My first friends were two cousins from Madrid, Mariam and Lucia, who invited me to go to the tailors with them (a speciality of Hội An). Together, we drank iced coconut coffees and sent candle-lit lanterns into the river, then sat drinking beers and watching the boats float by.

We talked about red flags (the ones that are international, and the ones that are specific to London and Madrid); about the tumultuous break-ups we'd cried over; and about the men who had lit a fire within us. We talked too about our jobs, and our ambitions, and our families, and our favourite countries and foods. We also bonded over that universal language: gossip. Like who was interested in whom in the hostel, and had it resulted in any bed-swapping? There was one thirty-five-year-old Aussie who provided endless fodder on that front.

The first time we spoke to him was over breakfast, when he was purchasing a copy of *Atomic Habits* from the hostel book stall. The three of us exchanged a look. It was a book that Mariam and Lucia had said was an instant red flag. He insisted that he wasn't there to meet girls; his trip was all about forming *connections*. He was *spiritual*. Although he worked a corporate job back home, his three weeks off in Asia were the time when he felt most like himself. Business at the front, believer at the back. Sure.

That night, it became obvious he was interested in a beautiful young American girl. She returned to his bed with him for the next few nights. Which would have been fine if it wasn't for what came next. The American girl left, and another American girl arrived. And we saw the Aussie guy have a remarkably similar conversation with the new girl: about how it was amazing to meet someone so far from home who felt so much like home. Actually, I think the words he chose were, 'a true connection'. But you get the point.

Anyway, he ended up sharing the same dorm bed with the same dirty sex sheets with this new girl less than twelve hours later. Did I mention we were in the same room? I woke up in the morning to hear the wet slurps of their intense kissing. Like nails across a chalkboard, but more intimate.

Then, he spoke in an attempted whisper that was a few decibels too loud, so the rest of the room could hear: 'One last kiss.' I wanted to barf. Thankfully a few moments later, he left the room to go and catch his plane.

I heard the door click and decided the coast was clear to get up and brush my teeth. But the woman he had been in bed with was still there, the curtain pulled back so that our eyes met.

'Ooops.' She giggled. 'He was just so sweet, I couldn't help myself.'

'It's okay, I didn't hear anything,' I lied.

'And it was his last night, of course it was. I wish we could have had more time.'

'Ah well, short but sweet.' I laughed awkwardly and made a swift exit. I knew she wanted me to sit there and swoon over him with her. To hear the details of what he'd said and the coincidences she couldn't explain. But I didn't have the heart to listen, knowing what I knew. I'd end up telling her and ruining her holiday romance. She didn't need that.

The thing that became glaringly obvious over the next few weeks was that most women love to talk about their love lives (okay, definitely guilty – even without writing a whole book on the topic) – and with those women, it's one of the fastest tracks to friendship intimacy. Asking, 'And are you single? Dating? In love? Have you broken any hearts, and has anyone broken yours?' immediately takes any surface-level chat to something much deeper.

It's why I had become close with the Spanish girls, and why I later developed friendships with a French woman called Marie, and an Australian woman called Mel, and an English woman called Laura, and a Spanish woman called Andrea. With all these women, we bonded over our relationships and situationships and friends-turned-lovers, and when we parted it felt like I had known them for far longer than just a couple of days. And that's because we didn't just get to know each other, we got to know each other's hearts. It connected us in a way that details about someone's job or where they live just doesn't. In many cases, we changed our plans to ensure our paths would cross again.

The Hà Giang Loop

I did not plan to go on this three-night motorbike trip in the very north of Vietnam. It was totally out of my comfort zone. But so many people had told me how incredible the experience was that I decided I would regret it if I didn't go. It helped that my new friends Marie and Mel from Hội An wanted to do it too, so we arranged to meet up again a week or so later to go together.

Marie and I took a long minibus ride from Hanoi to Hà Giang, where Mel was waiting for us at a hostel. She warned us over WhatsApp that it wasn't quite as inviting as it had looked online. The pool was a murky green colour (and clearly had not been used in months), and the single dorm room was packed with beds, all creaky, with no curtains and thin sheets. None of us slept well that night, and in the morning we woke to the sound of rain. The forecast looked dire. Not exactly ideal for spending your day outside rushing along hairpin bends on a motorbike.

But the next few days were some of the most magical I have ever experienced: we spent them zooming up and down mountains to be met with incredible views. The rain and the mist only added to the mystery of the place, and on the last day we had beautiful blue skies. Every night we did karaoke with our new motley crew (a mix of Dutch, American, Austrian, Scottish, French, Australian and more, with fifteen or so Vietnamese men as our guides) and would toast the day with rounds of 'happy water' (a local rice wine, home-made and served out of plastic bottles). Together we would chant cheers, *'Mot, Hai, Ba, Yo!'*

I fancied several of the men, as did Marie. Mel kept her cards closer to her chest. But the one man I ended up liking the most – well, I would never have ended up sleeping with him, if it wasn't for the little black dog that bit me on the first night.

I had decided to pet the dog because I was tipsy, but when I turned around to head back to the others, it chased me and jumped up, biting my ankles and wrists. There was the tiniest break of the skin. I wasn't hurt, but suddenly my anxiety spiralled. I googled cases of rabies in Vietnam, and that didn't help. I ended up crying in front of lots of people, which wasn't the first impression I had hoped for (red and puffy-faced and catastrophising).

One of the sorry few who bore witness to my meltdown was Xuan. He was one of the drivers on our tour, and we hadn't interacted much before then. He was definitely the clown of the group, though, pushing his face up against the glass of a window to pull a silly expression and opting for dramatic poses in each group photo. We'd nicknamed him 'Wild Card' because he was also a bit of a daredevil, doing tricks on his bike and flips off rocks. His English was better than many of the others', and he tried to console me by pulling up his trousers to show me his own legs, which were covered in dog bites. 'See, I'm alive!' he said. I kept crying.

I called Shreya back home, relying on her advice as a doctor. She told me in no uncertain terms I should get it checked out, even if it meant cancelling the motorbike trip. In the morning, I went to a local pharmacy, and they said that though the chances were small, I should get an injection. And so off to a very remote local hospital I went. The doctor spoke no English and held up a picture of a rabid-looking dog foaming at the mouth, before plunging a syringe into my arm. Throughout the rest of the trip, it gave Xuan an excuse to come over to me at the different viewpoints and tease me. How do you flirt when you can't communicate much? The answer is all in the body language. He bit my leg, he barked from behind me; I gently shoved him back.

On the final night, it became obvious we liked each other. There was an energy to the evening from the off, because throughout the trip we'd all been talking about the final night's pool party.

The only negative? There was a scary-looking dog chained to the wall outside when we checked in to our hostel. The dog itself wasn't necessarily scary, but the heavy chain made him look more menacing. And understandably, since the dog-bite incident, I was less laissez-faire and a little more freaked out about being near any animal. Dogs, bats, you name it.

The first thing everyone did was get cold beers from the fridge and strip off into swimsuits to jump into the huge pool. It felt like such a luxury after a long day on the bike in the sun, with dirt and dust coating our skin. There was music playing, and it felt like a proper party. The drivers joined in, bombing into the pool to see who could make the biggest splash.

Xuan started to play-fight with me in the water, pulling me under the surface. I'd see him out of the corner of my eye, swimming over, deep under the water. Then suddenly he'd pull my foot down, like a shark I had to look out for. Except that I liked it. I'd splash water into his face when we surfaced.

At one point, while I was perching on the side of the pool, with my feet dangling in, Xuan swam over and positioned himself under my legs with his arms wrapped around them. Then he started to massage my feet. I could see Marie and Mel go wide-eyed on the other side of the pool, tilting their heads to the side and giggling together.

Abruptly, he asked, 'Are you married?'

I was glad he wasn't facing me so he couldn't see the expression of surprise on my face. 'No.'

He continued, 'Do you have a boyfriend?'

'No.'

'Good.'

I laughed. 'Do you have a girlfriend?'

He laughed too. 'No.'

We stayed there for a while.

Later, he said, 'I will go shower,' and disappeared. I left the pool too to get changed, slipping on a little black dress.

'Nice,' said Mel with a wink.

'Dressing up?' said Marie.

'Noooo. Maybe. It is a pool party.' I spun round.

We left the room together for our final dinner. I looked around the table at the faces that had become like family. Xuan led us in the final round of 'happy water'. After dinner, we played a game kicking a shuttlecock around. Xuan was there, and I felt a little shy around him for the first time.

Then someone unchained the dog and he started roaming around. The dog wandered over and I visibly flinched.

Xuan asked, 'Why are you scared? You do not like dogs?'

'No, I do, but you know – the bite kind of put me off.'

He looked confused, whether it was because he couldn't understand what I'd said, or because he couldn't see why that would put me off, I wasn't sure.

'Look, safe,' and he petted the dog. Then he took my hand and helped me to pet the dog too. I continued to pet it despite every bone in my body telling me not to. This is when I knew I definitely liked Xuan. It's amazing the fears you can overcome when you want someone to like you. An upside-down roller coaster? Normally: no. But if the person in question likes them and will hold my hand: absolutely.

We started to use Google Translate on his phone to talk more. I learned he was an only child. He told me about working on the Loop, and his dreams of setting up on his own one day. He told me about the stories behind his tattoos. He had travelled a lot in Vietnam and gave me recommendations.

Much later on, he asked, 'Have you been sleeping well?'

'Okay, considering how many people are in the room,' I replied.

'I have my own room.' He gave me a knowing smile.

I can confirm that this was a bit of an exaggeration: yes, it was a double bed compared to my single, and yes, there were curtains that went round it, but there were also seven other beds like his in the room. That didn't put me off. We started slowly, peeling off each layer of our clothes in turn like a game of pass-the-parcel in between drawn-out kisses, gradually becoming faster and faster. The sex was magnificent. I was in ecstasy.

Anyone else on our tour could tell you that. And it wasn't because they heard us (thank goodness for the loud music downstairs), but because later, when we went back to the party, I could not wipe the smile off my face. Several people told me my huge grin for the next hour or two gave it away that something had happened.

So, while the incident with that little black dog was incredibly stressful, I guess there was a silver lining.

The next morning, Xuan playfully swung my hand back and forth as we walked away from the bikes. I knew he wasn't meant to sleep with a guest, and so I felt a bit awkward in front of his colleagues, but it soon subsided. One of the last stops on our way back to the first hostel, where an overnight bus was waiting to take us tourists back to Hanoi, was a gorgeous waterfall. Xuan kept doing backflips off the rocks; I couldn't help but be impressed, if not a little scared for him.

'Have you noticed . . .?' Mel asked me.

'What?'

'Xuan's got scratches on his back. I wonder why.' She smirked.

'No idea. Poor guy,' I said.

Xuan said goodbye with a hug and a kiss on the cheek just before I hopped on the bus. I knew it was unlikely we would stay in touch, and there was a good chance he might have had romances with other girls on the Loop before. But I didn't mind, as long as I didn't know. I had been happy in the moment with him, and he had been with me. That was all that mattered. Some romances aren't meant to last, and the inevitable fleetingness only adds to the allure.

For my last few weeks in Vietnam, I continued to travel with some others from the group, including Saar, a man with one of the most optimistic outlooks I have ever met. We journeyed to Ha Long Bay together, where we splashed out on a bougie boat trip; it felt like we were about to take part in a murder mystery with all the different characters on board. Over dinner, he told me about his Grindr escapades and how he makes a nice memory in each place; it was his version of collecting a fridge magnet. Later, we met up with a few of the Dutch and Austrians from our group in Ninh Bình. It was like being reunited with old friends, and we floated along rivers in rowing boats and did yet more karaoke on top of a double-decker bus.

Canggu

I was excited to fly to Bali, not only to see a new place, but because my sister was going to visit me. It's only a six-hour flight from Melbourne.

I knew there was also a chance that I might see Max, but I hadn't factored him into my plans; remember, the last time we met, we had left things firmly as friends.

But then a funny thing happened. On my first night in Seminyak, a couple of hours after I arrived, I got a message from Max at 5.42pm:

> Hey. Where did you get info on boats for Gili?
> Feel like going out tonight?

We had spoken briefly on the phone the week before, suggesting that if our paths crossed, we should go for drinks. The most likely place seemed to be the Gili Islands; he hadn't said he planned to spend any time on the main island of Bali at all. He'd actually said he intended not to. So I'd had no idea he would be nearby. Was it the fact I was going to be there that had altered his plans? I couldn't help but wonder. I asked where he was staying, and he told me he was in Canggu. It was twenty-five minutes away by motorbike.

I went back and forth in my mind over whether to go. I had planned to have a chilled night to make sure I was rested for when Kate arrived the next day. If I knew anything about my sister,

it was that we had a lot of fun nights out ahead of us. And if I
wanted to keep up with her, I needed to be ready. I didn't have a
SIM card yet, and it was already late.

He texted again:

> I can give you the name of our restaurant and
> not move until you arrive.

I asked Kate what to do. 'Oh my god, you should go!' she told
me. Kate is so much better at not overthinking things. If there's
a small possibility something will be fun, she'll go for it. And her
magic power is that she can always make it fun, even if it's not. I
try to channel that energy whenever I can. In fact, I often think,
What would Kate do? She may be younger than me but she is wise.
And less uptight.

I texted Max:

> Okay, I am on my way.

I met him and his friend Gabriel (whom I'd also met on the
ski trip) on the main strip, and then we headed straight into an
outdoor bar-meets-club called Old Man's. We drank craft beers
and then mixed drinks, and weaved our way through the crowd
until we were near the DJ. It was fun and friendly. I didn't feel out
of place with them both; they warmly welcomed me in.

I kept stealing glances of Max bopping to the beat with his
kooky, uninhibited energy. It made me nostalgic. We had danced
together on the ski trip, and I wanted him to take my hand and
swirl me around again. That said, the heavy bass wouldn't have
been quite right for that.

The club closed at 1am and so we got one last drink each from
the bar and took them with us to sit on the beach. Gabriel had
left an hour earlier, so it was just me and Max. It was pure chaos
outside, makeshift tattoo stalls with drunk people choosing

designs haphazardly, and more loud live music coming from who knows where, and lots of motorbikes trying to chug through. We disappeared down a quiet side street until we ended up at the beach, and then wandered along the sand until we found a piece of driftwood to sit on.

The sea was dramatic that night, with the waves rolling in, crashing far out and then in again and again, closer to the shore. It felt surreal to be sitting there next to Max. It was the third time we'd met in eight months or so, each occasion in a different location. And each time, it had been by complete chance we'd been in the same place at the same time. I couldn't quite believe it, but I also had a sense that it couldn't have unfolded in any other way.

The conversation was light, and flirty. Then I said, 'This feels different to Bordeaux.'

'It does,' he said.

'I thought maybe it was just a holiday romance. We felt just like friends, nothing more.'

'Hmm,' he said.

'What do you think?'

'Yeah, I thought the same.'

'And now?'

'Different.'

Neither of us could put our finger on why. I thought the fact I had changed the plans at the last minute back in Bordeaux had not helped. He'd probably thought I wasn't interested. And so we both held back.

'It's so funny to see you again, and on the other side of the world,' I said. 'I didn't think we would ever see each other again.'

'I did,' he said. 'You didn't?'

'No. Really?'

'Yeah, I did. I'm not surprised.'

We kissed. Then we both had a wee in the sand (separately, not in some sexy way) and walked back towards his hostel holding hands.

'I'd like to stay over, but I'm not having sex,' I said.

'Oh really?' He thought I was joking.

'I've heard my fair share of night-time noises on this trip in hostels and I don't want to be the culprit.' In my head, I added 'again', but didn't say that part out loud.

We fell asleep in his bunk. We had never actually slept side by side. It felt natural.

In the morning, I woke to Gabriel's voice. In French, he said, 'Max, we need to get going and check out.'

Max replied, 'Lizzie is here.'

Gabriel didn't believe him.

I poked my head out from behind the curtain. 'Hi Gabriel.'

He laughed.

I checked my phone and realised it wouldn't be long before my sister arrived. Max walked me to the front of the hostel and waited with me while I ordered a Grab to take me home. When the Grab driver arrived, Max hugged me, then leaned down for a kiss (he is a foot taller than me). It was nice, but the PDA still felt a bit much in broad daylight, and so I quickly grabbed the spare helmet and hopped on to the bike.

The driver asked loudly, 'Is this your boyfriend?'

I looked at Max and said, 'Yes.' I don't know why. It just felt right, and I didn't panic afterwards about what Max might think. That's not to say in any way that he actually was my boyfriend, just that I felt comfortable enough to call him that while we were in the same place. My Bali boyfriend.

We continued to message over the next few days, and I realised that I wanted to see him again.

Gili Trawangan

Meanwhile, Kate and I were having the best reunion on Gili T. The island is actually closer to neighbouring Lombok, and about a ninety-minute boat ride from Bali. It's known for being a party island, but there are also incredible white-sand beaches and turtles swimming just offshore, and some of the most richly coloured sunsets I have ever seen. We fell into a routine of sunbathing and swimming, before returning to our hostel to change, then going out for seafood skewers in the market and dancing on tables in bars.

We had one argument. It involved me trying to buy a bikini. All my swimsuits were falling apart, thanks to having spent the last six weeks in humid climates, dipping in and out of oceans and pools. And I had got myself worked up, wanting to have something cute for when I next saw Max. I ended up buying the tiniest little red bikini ever. They didn't have the next size up, and I panicked and spent way too much money. When I tried it on for my sister later, she told me point blank it was too small and not flattering. I knew she was right. That annoyed me even more. We yelled at each other, and then she said I could wear the bottoms of her bikini. This is how sisters work: fighting one minute, borrowing each other's clothes the next.

Together, we cycled all around the island in the dark, and we stopped at a very hippie bar. Most people were on shrooms, and trance music was blasting out of the speakers. There was a woman hula-hooping by the fire. I asked Kate if she would mind staying an extra day so that I could see Max again, and she could meet him too. We were meant to leave the day before he was getting there. She said, 'Of course we can stay another night.' We danced into the early hours and went for a night-time dip.

The next day I messaged Max to formulate a plan. He replied:

> Sounds great! We'll rent bikes from our hotel I guess and meet somewhere there. Plus Gabriel is being Gabriel and has brought girls with him. They're nice though. You'll meet them! Plus I need to find him a gift for his birthday tonight. Any ideas?

My heart sank. I panicked that maybe one of the girls they were travelling with fancied Max and was hoping something would happen – or worse, maybe something already had happened on Nusa Penida, where they had been previously. I knew I didn't have any right to feel jealous, but I did. I told my sister.

She rightly put me in my place. 'He doesn't owe you anything. If we get there and that's the situation, we'll go do something else.'

Again, she is much better at looking at love through a practical lens. At least when it comes to *my* dating life.

Just as we were about to leave to meet Max, a beautiful Dutch man walked up the stairs to our room. He had a deep tan and sun-bleached tousled hair from months of travelling on his own. His name was Coen. I saw it as an opportunity. If Max was going to bring women, I would bring this beautiful man. That would show him – or so I thought.

I asked, 'Do you want to come with us? We're about to go to a pool with a sunset view.'

'Oh – are you sure I won't be intruding, if you two are sisters?'

'No, we're actually going to meet a group. It's kind of a long story, but I met some of them in France earlier this year.'

'Great. I will come.'

Together, we cycled over to the other side of the island. We got there first and went for a dip in the pool. Max and Gabriel and the girls arrived not long after, and it didn't take long to realise I had nothing to worry about. It was clear nothing had happened between them, and Max started flirting with me almost immediately, pulling me to sit on his knee.

At one point the Dutch man took me aside. 'I think that French guy fancies you.'

'I know,' I said. 'There's some history there.'

'Ahhh, I see.' He was happy for me as I filled him in. He told me he was also a fan of love stories that cross continents. He'd had a fling with an Italian man in Rome whom he'd ended up bumping into in Bali too.

Meanwhile, Kate and Max had been jumping off a series of extremely high diving boards. I was too scared to do it, but with some convincing from Max, we went and did it together. Admittedly, not from the highest one. What was that about feeling brave when you like someone? Or is it just that you are more likely to do stupid things in the hope of impressing them?

While I was chatting to Gabriel, trying to seem casual, I said, 'Max said you're in a homestay. Is it nice? Are you in the same room or separate rooms?' I thought I wasn't being too obvious.

He saw right through it. Rather than replying, he shouted over to Max, 'Max, Lizzie wants to know if we have separate rooms.'

I splashed him with water.

We had berry mojitos and watched the sun turn the same colour as our drinks. I had been nervous for Kate to meet Max, but she told me she liked him. I breathed a sigh of relief. My family's opinions of who I like are incredibly important to me, especially as I know I've pursued some absolute fucking weasels. Berks, twerps, you name it. And in the past, I haven't always listened to my family's advice. I wouldn't make that mistake again.

We all went out to dinner together and then rolled from one bar to another, looking for the next round of rum and Cokes. At midnight, we sang happy birthday to Gabriel. At one point, Max and Gabriel wandered off. Kate and I were dancing on a table under a disco ball hanging from the wooden lean-to ceiling. I asked her if we should follow them?

She said, 'No, they'll come back.'

'But what if they don't?'

'They will.'

And she was right. When Max returned, he was easy to spot because he is so tall. At one point he stood still and shouted upwards, 'Lizzie, where are you? I miss you.' He was drunk, but still – my heart melted. Kate shook her head in laughter. Eventually, we kissed.

That night was the first time Max and I had an entire bedroom to ourselves (no, the yoga room where we could have been walked in on at any moment does not count). As soon as we were alone, he raised his eyebrows at me, and I mock-blushed. He picked me up and jumped through the air on to the bed. We were happy.

Nusa Penida, Uluwatu and Ubud

Kate and I travelled to Nusa Penida, by boat. It took four hours to reach the island, far longer than it was meant to, and the water was incredibly choppy. Max texted me within a couple of hours to ask if we'd made the boat and how it had all gone. His texting behaviour was so different to other men I have dated; he always replied quickly and often double-messaged. We continued chatting for the rest of the time, and I had a feeling we would see each other again. Where? I wasn't sure yet. And I was perfectly content with that.

Over the next week or so, Kate and I hiked down crazy steep paths to beautiful beaches I'd only ever dreamed of, learned how to surf with local instructors, and boogied our hearts out.

I was sad when she left, as I didn't know when we would see each other again. I cried ferociously as she got into her taxi. As I walked back into reception, Kate texted me:

> The taxi driver thinks you're in love with me.

The taxi driver wasn't wrong. I am madly in love with my sister. People reserve the phrase 'in love' for romance, but I think they're wrong to do that.

I knew there were just a few weeks left of my adventure and I was determined to make the most of them.

I headed to the beach hotspot of Uluwatu, where I met up with Marie, my French friend from Vietnam, and we both spent our days working by the pool: Marie on her business, and me on the very beginning bones of this book. By night, we'd party with rugged surfers, dancing to live music. One night, Marie spotted a man. She shoved me and said, 'Look at him.' But as we approached she quickly spun round. 'Abort; he's wearing Crocs.'

At the end of the week I decided to travel to Ubud with Laura, who I'd also met in Vietnam. We'd stayed connected, and wanted to spend time together again.

When it came to deciding where to meet up this time, we both were drawn to Ubud. I had spent most of my time in Bali by the sea; I felt it was time to go inland to cycle along spectacular terraced rice fields, hike up volcanoes, and learn about intricate Hindu temples and shrines.

What I hadn't fully thought through beforehand was that Laura had been doing a 200-hour yoga teacher-training course since I'd last seen her, and the main reason she wanted to go to Ubud was to experiment with all different forms of the practice. I knew somewhere in the corner of my mind that yoga was a reason people visited Ubud, but I hadn't fully realised how much of a centre it was. As we drove into the city, we saw that every other traveller had a yoga mat slung over their shoulder. I could see the excitement in Laura's eyes. To her, this was Disneyland.

She looked up the schedules for a few places on her phone. 'Oh, there is a Kundalini we might be able to make later. Or Hatha tomorrow at 7am? Or a Vinyasa Flow a bit later? Oooh, we could do both?'

I didn't know what any of these words meant, and I certainly had no desire to get up at 6am for a class.

'Um, it feels like sacrilege to say this here . . . but I don't really like yoga.'

This was true; I had tried it a smattering of times with friends who raved about it, but I always came away feeling a bit disinterested, unsure what I was missing. I didn't have much time to exercise back at home, and I wanted to sweat and feel a rush of endorphins if I was going to move my body.

Laura stared at me wide-eyed and then laughed.

I added quickly: 'I'll definitely come to one class. But I can't see myself doing more than one in a day.'

'Okay, deal,' she replied.

That afternoon we decided to stroll around the town, stopping in different shops to look at beautiful clothes, quirky trinkets, and finally books. I needed a new one and there were a few English-language shops. I picked up hardback novels with bright covers I recognised from Instagram, mulling over which one to choose. Then, out of the corner of my eye, I spotted a big display of Elizabeth Gilbert's *Eat Pray Love*. I picked up a copy and showed it to Laura. 'I've actually never read this, but it would be embarrassing to read it here, right?'

I knew very little about the book – other than the fact it was a memoir about an American woman who goes to Italy, India and Indonesia to find herself – and had only ever watched the film half-asleep on a plane.

'What? You've never read it? It's a classic.' She smiled.

'I guess if I'm ever going to read it, this is the place.' I knew a large chunk of it was set in Ubud and the surrounding villages.

'Get it! Honestly, I'm pretty excited for you; I wish I could read it for the first time again,' Laura said.

That night, we went for drinks and got deeper into our lives and our friendship. Laura shared with me the things that had brought her to yoga back in England – and told me how much it had helped her. That's why she had wanted to press pause on her corporate job and see if she could make yoga a bigger part of her day-to-day. She told me about a long relationship she'd ended, and a work romance that she wasn't yet ready to leave behind.

In the morning, we did our first yoga class at the Yoga Barn. It's by far the biggest studio in the town (there are at least a dozen others) with close to thirty classes a day spread around in different buildings. Some have huge windows looking out on to streams, jungle plants and statues; others are open to the elements. There are lots of quiet nooks with wooden day beds where you can sit and read a book, and you'll often see people practising acroyoga in the main courtyard. An elaborate mandala is made with flowers each day, and yet more fresh blossoms are slung in garlands over a central statue of Ganesh.

Our Vinyasa Flow class (where poses are linked together with the breath in a sequence) was full, meaning there were nearly a hundred of us in the great wooden space. We could hear the noises of the birds in the trees rustling outside, and as we moved into Warrior One pose, I spotted geckos inching across the ceiling. It was partly because of this incredible setting that, for the first time, I felt like I might *get it*. I wasn't fully there yet, but I was starting to see how this could bring something beneficial to your life. It wasn't just the setting, though; there was something about the fact we were such a huge mass of people all moving in sync. Online reviews I'd read beforehand said there were too many people in the class, but that was precisely why I liked it.

We'd only booked to stay in Ubud for three nights, but quickly Laura and I decided to extend for a couple more. We went to a few more yoga classes, but we also walked through beautiful rice fields, ate incredibly messy and smoky and delicious ribs and did a sunrise hike up Mount Batur, where the pitch black in front of us receded to slowly reveal an epic landscape. We spotted countless monkeys on street corners and up telephone poles, and they had such serious expressions that they looked like they were pondering the meaning of life. Every day was hot and sunny and blue-skied.

We tried a Kundalini class, which included a long segment where everyone had to laugh at the same time. I adored it. It felt liberating, a return to childlike wonder. I wanted to do more of it. Afterwards, Laura told me she hadn't enjoyed it.

'What? I loved it.' I was surprised.

'You're becoming a bigger yogi than me,' she said.

All the while, I was reading *Eat Pray Love* – and Laura was right, I was enraptured by it. The similarities were spooky too. I guess I was looking for them. First off, the author is called Elizabeth, like me, which seems obvious, but I hadn't noticed it before. Then there's the fact she was also in her thirties, that it was also September when she visited Bali, and that she also felt so lucky to be given the chance to travel on her own instead of in a couple. She travelled often for magazine assignments to write articles, which was why she'd ended up in Bali the first time, but she decided to go back to experience it on her own without any sort of pre-planning. She would just see what happened when she got there – just like I had. When I counted back the years to her visit, I realised it had been exactly two decades since she first came to Bali, and yet so much still resonated.

The longer we stayed in Ubud and the more I read of the book, the more I really started to embrace yoga, and a spiritual mentality, and the wonderfully woo-woo. And so when Laura decided it was time to move on to the islands and then perhaps Lombok, I decided to stay. I knew there were so many more places I could visit, and part of me felt like I was failing, knowing I would have been in Bali for a whole month and not have made it to Nusa Lembongan or Lombok or Flores or many more places. But I was happy in Ubud, and I knew there was more for me there. What's more, I wanted to do it on my own. I felt I needed to do it on my own.

When Laura left, I decided to move to a homestay with my own room to really allow me to spend time by myself. I had realised it was impossible to do this in a hostel when everyone was coming and going. I had been afraid of not meeting people at the beginning of my trip, but with just ten days left to go, I realised I wanted nothing more than to have time for myself. I knew too that I didn't want to meet any more love interests. Elizabeth Gilbert swore off men for a year; that sounded like something I wanted to do. She wasn't successful in that plan, falling for an unexpected Brazilian man in Ubud before her twelve months were up; I think I lasted about six weeks. But the intention was there. I knew, as Elizabeth wrote in her memoir, that 'healing and peace can only come from being on your own'.

I wanted to explore other parts of the Yoga Barn: sound baths and meditations and journaling sessions and more. I signed up for something called a 'Heart Journey'. If I'd done this in London, I might have found it all a bit too cheesy and spiritual, but instead I found myself taking notes and nodding along.

The leader, Rodolfo, was very engaging, encouraging the group to connect through just one word or a symbol. By this point, I had realised that most women who travel solo to Bali aren't just there for a holiday. It's often for a deeper purpose, to look into their hearts and heal. To see what might be missing, or to realise that nothing was ever missing. To understand that they are enough on their own. I call it the *Eat Pray Love* effect.

And so the women in this room were all ears, listening intently to what Rodolfo had to say. He began by telling us that our romantic lives are like a closet. We have to get rid of stuff to make space for the new. Because the longer we entertain what's not for us, the longer we postpone what is. It was obvious to me that I hadn't ever followed this rule. I have rarely had clean breaks in relationships, and frequently wonder 'What if?' This has often led to me revisiting situations or relationships – whether that's one mistaken kiss or something more significant – but the outcome has never been any different the second time round. More often than not, it's ended up way messier. I realised Rodolfo was right. Going forwards, I had to cut contact to move on. I wasn't going to find the right person when I hadn't properly closed the door on all the others.

Of course, social media makes this harder, because it allows us to keep tabs on people. In the first weeks after you go your separate ways, it can be easy to become obsessed with it, because it's the only intel you have on how they are coping. If you're anything like me, you'll have put yourself through the torment of waiting a long time (okay, thirteen minutes and thirty-seven seconds) to watch an Instagram story in an effort to not seem too keen, only to be met with an uninteresting picture of a cup of coffee on a desk and an empty feeling. It's just a stupid picture. It doesn't give you any insight into how they are feeling or what they are doing or whether they might get back in touch. The best way to rip off the plaster is to delete them completely, but if you can't bear to do that, you can at the very least hide their stories. You have to make space for the unknown.

He also told us that manifesting isn't a magical thing; it's simply the act of giving ourselves permission. I still repeat this to myself now. You have to know what you want in order to get it, and there's no shortcut to finding out – you need to spend that time on your own to figure out exactly what it is you really want. And once you know what that is, you have to share it with the people around you. Even if that's scary. Even if you think it could lead to embarrassment. This applies to career goals and ambitions, but also to romance. I've hidden my feelings for a man too many times, only to be frustrated down the line when they didn't want the same thing. I could have spared myself the pain, or at the very least had a better idea of what I was letting myself in for before getting emotionally too deep.

On another evening, I decided to do a class on ecstatic dance. There were twenty of us in the room, men and women of all nationalities and ages. Our teacher was from Java and had been in Bali for twelve years. He started by showing us several different ways to move one small part of our bodies, before focusing on another and another. There were no concrete rules, though; you could dance however you wanted. The instructions were just to make everyone feel more comfortable. The real joy came when you could freestyle and whirl wildly around the room. I spun round in tight circles, leaped from one spot to another, fell to the floor to crawl along, and then slowly stood again to twist my body this way and that. It reminded me of how I used to dance when I was younger. Not afraid to put a foot wrong, not held back by embarrassment. I left feeling lighter, and on my walk back to the homestay, I did a Google search to see if there would be another opportunity to do it again before I left.

By chance, there was a supermoon that weekend, and with it an all-day al fresco festival of ecstatic dancing. It felt fortuitous. I had never been to a festival on my own, and it was hard to tell from the event's website exactly what would be in store at this one. There was lots of trippy-hippie language, calling the guests 'cosmic wanderers' and inviting us to 'celebrate the power of the moon in this phase'. There would be music and dancing, yes, but what was a cacao ceremony? I wasn't sure what to wear or whether I would fit in. There was also a warning that your clothes had to stay on at all times; the fact they said this made me wonder what exactly I was signing up for.

But I booked a ticket and decided the hardest part would be arriving on my own. It could only get easier after that, and no one knew me here anyway. If I didn't like it or I didn't feel I fitted in, I could leave.

The cacao ceremony was first on the agenda, so at least I'd figure out what that was. The courtyard was filled with a couple of hundred people, dressed in a mixture of yoga wear and back-packing clothes (you know, floaty tie-dye trousers and crop tops, that sort of thing; I'd gone for the latter).

I noticed a French man in his forties or fifties who looked like a wizard, wearing a dramatic black outfit that was decorated with thunderbolts and had a plunging neckline. He had a matching headscarf and gold bangles. But it wasn't necessarily the outfit that caught my eye, it was his energy. Everyone was gravitating towards him, and his expression was spirited and engaged.

It wasn't a surprise, then, when he turned out to be the one leading us through the cacao ceremony. He began by telling the group to move in large circles around the space.

'Now, normally, when we get to a party, we turn to alcohol to open ourselves to new connections, to let loose. But today we aren't drinking, so let's try something different.' He flashed a wicked smile.

I hadn't realised this would be a sober event, but I was ready to lean into it. I had no other choice.

At regular intervals, our French wizard man would shout, 'Stop.' And then, 'Now look at the person in front of you, really look at them. Take their hands in yours. Repeat after me: I see you. I hear you. I love you. You are beautiful. I am here for you. Now hug.' And then we would begin again.

It was difficult to maintain such prolonged eye contact with people I had never met. But it wasn't difficult to say the words, because we were all chanting them together. Somehow, I didn't feel ridiculous for saying 'I love you' to a stranger at all. I mean, they were saying it back to me. At one point, I spotted a woman, Andrea, whom I'd met a month earlier in Vietnam.

'What are you doing here?' she mouthed across the circle, waving at me.

I didn't reply, just grinned and gestured around me as if it was obvious. Why would you *not* want to be here?

The ceremony also included drinking a cup of rich and bitter cacao. During this part, various people went to the centre of our circle to shout something that meant something to them. Each time, we all chanted 'Jaya!' It was impossible not to feel connected to the others in the circle.

The rest of the night passed too quickly. The smell of incense was everywhere, there were several stages with incredible live music, and hours and hours of ecstatic dancing. Of course, every time you looked up to the sky, you would see the supermoon. It was so big and bright that it almost looked fake. Everyone was barefoot and moving exactly as they wanted to. There were some people who had such skill and rhythm, it was hard not to stop and be entranced by their bodies. It would have been easy to feel jealous, but I never did. Instead, I just felt such contentment, I wanted to bottle the feeling and hold on to it. That way, I could release a little of it every time I felt less than good enough in the future. Every time I needed a reminder of how it was possible to feel. We dance like this as kids, then we forget, and we have to relearn it. On my way home, I realised that I had never felt so comfortable with myself, in my body and with being alone. And I hadn't had a sip of alcohol. I had to find a way to remember this in my bones.

I couldn't go to sleep in the homestay, because my energy was sky high. Instead, I bounced around the room, dancing and singing to myself.

I sent a voice note to Max: 'It's weird, because there was no alcohol or anything, and I haven't drunk anything, but I kind of *feel* drunk. It was amazing. All this amazing live music, and dancing. And I tried acroyoga, and it turns out I'm a natural.'

'Lizzie, I think it's time to come home,' he replied.

Of course, I did have to go home. And I did so, a few days later. As the plane took off, the pilot made an announcement: 'If you look out of your window now, you'll see a volcano erupting.'

He was right, I could see the golden magma spilling out of the top; it was easy to spot when everything else was either night sky or landscapes shrouded in darkness.

On the long journey home, I thought about the various highs and lows of my trip. There had definitely been both. And I'm not just talking about the dog bite. I had cried at a couple of points early on, not knowing what to do next and feeling unsure of myself. But I had also had the adventure of a lifetime and met so many kindred spirits. I felt lucky to have had this chance, not just to travel for a few months, but to have been able to do it on my own. Because the important thing was that I had truly learned how to be on my own. Not just in the sense of not being in a relationship, but also in terms of managing without my support network around me. The second part was far harder. It was a reminder of the importance of the people who listen and laugh and advise and console me – and what they offer me every day. I hope they feel I offer the same in return.

And so I came home with a full heart, open to all kinds of love – romantic and platonic. One of these kinds of love I need, and the other I want. I'm not afraid to say that – I do want to find romantic love again – but I know I don't *need* it.

Because despite having been burned, having had my heart ripped into little pieces time and time again, I still believe it's worth putting yourself out there. It's part of the magic of rom-coms, that no matter what happens, our heroine never gives up hope. That often the lesson is that the right person will love you exactly as you are, even with all your quirks. The fact you put gallons of tahini on everything, the fact you watch the same Spanish telenovela over and over again, the fact you sometimes speak too quickly without thinking, the fact you are always five minutes late. In fact, they will love you not in spite of these quirks, but *because* of them.

And so, more than ever, I'm determined to make that search fun and silly and magic. To remember that the journey to love is meant to bring us joy. It can be easy to forget that.

The number of single friends who have had a first date and said to me, 'It was fun, but I'm trying not to get too excited yet,' is far too high.

Hell, I've said it myself.

It was only recently I realised how sad that is.

My close friend Nick sent me an eight-minute – yes, eight-minute – voice note following an excellent date, one with connection, and mutual attraction, where they had talked all night, but then followed it up with a message that said: 'And now I need to just calm down, and not get in my own head, and not overthink it.' I knew exactly what they meant: that they had been burned before and didn't want to get their hopes up yet.

But I also realised that this is completely the wrong way to look at it. We have to go into a new romance with open hearts and open minds. If we go in thinking the worst, then what can we expect but that? If we feel excited, we should act excited.

'Allow yourself to feel exactly how you are feeling,' I told them. 'This is one of the best parts of dating, and by dialling down the volume on it, you're only taking away the fun. It will either work out or it won't; being excited about it won't change that likelihood.'

Nick said: 'I needed to hear this. I love you. I will let myself feel what I really feel.'

You may have noticed that this chapter didn't star a leading man, even though there were a few cameo appearances. But I've learned that they aren't the main character. I am.

And so are you.

Some things I've learned about love

- ♥ Love can be slurping spaghetti off the same plate, licking tomato sauce off each other's faces.

- ♥ It can be realising your ex's best friend was the one all along.

- ♥ It can be booking a last-minute flight and seeing who can eat more pastel de nata in one weekend.

- ♥ It can be watching them hang out the washing for the umpteenth time.

- ♥ It can be pressing the emergency stop button in the elevator to have sex right then and there.

- ♥ It can happen at any time. That is to say, there is no deadline.

- ♥ It can be straight out of a romcom. It can be a meet-cute and a story for the grandkids, for the ages.

- ♥ It can be heartbreaking. It can be crying down the phone to whoever will listen.

- ♥ It can be platonic and powerful and essential.

- ♥ It can be driving down the highway with your dad, music blaring.

- ♥ It can be slurping oysters with your mum.

- ♥ It can be dancing on tables with your sister.

- ♥ It can be swimming in the sea on a freezing day with your friends.

- ♥ It can be all things.

- ♥ It can make you feel the highest of highs, and the lowest of lows.

- ♥ And somehow, despite everything, your heart will find a way to welcome it, again and again.

AUTHOR'S NOTE

This is a book about my life and how I remember it. It is non-fiction, yes, but through my own lens. I know that memories can shapeshift as time goes on, and many of the stories are from years ago, but I have done my best to tell them as they were, to remember the good and the bad in equal measure. I used diaries, Facebook messages, playlists, WhatsApps, photo albums and voice notes to transport me back to those times; I spoke to friends and family who were there to get their takes and to remind me of details I had forgotten, much like they do in my day-to-day life when I call them to get their advice on a date or a decision (romantic or otherwise).

I know that particularly when it comes to the love interests in this book, everyone will have their own version of events. Each will have a different story where they are the main character, and I am just a supporting role. It is why I have changed the names and identifying details of some people, especially those who are no longer a big part of my life. I hope that if they read this book, they can understand me a little better and know that I am grateful for each relationship, situationship, one-night stand and somewhere-in-between that has got me here.

Indeed, a surprising side effect of writing this book was not only seeing how much I've grown and how I've become the woman I am today, but also finding a definitive closure that I didn't know was possible. I've learned a lot about what I want, and what I need, and what I can offer someone. I also know what

I won't accept, which is just as important. It's been wild to see some of the patterns I've followed again and again in relationships and realise what I've got to change. That's not to say I have it all figured out, but I know more than I did aged fifteen. Thank goodness.

ACKNOWLEDGEMENTS

Thank you to my agent Millie Lean. I felt a connection with you from the very first time we met and am so grateful that you believed in this book when it was just a couple of chapters. You helped me to believe in myself. You are a huge talent and the best cheerleader.

Thank you to my editor Bernadette Marron. Your edits made me both laugh and cry happy tears. You have helped me enormously to shape this book into what it is; I can't imagine doing it with anyone other than you. Plus I love that you love romcoms as much as me.

Thank you to my publicist Gaby Drinkald for being so enthusiastic from the start. I have loved all of your ideas, and, of course, the fact that your cover photo on Twitter is the Bridget Jones book launch scene.

Thank you to the teams at YMU and Piatkus that have contributed so many ideas and championed this book. I feel so fortunate to have such incredible people on my side. Sarah Thomas; Tara O'Sullivan; Charlotte Stroomer; Louise Harvey; Kirsty Howarth.

Thank you to Claire Irvin for commissioning me to write an article about recreating *The Holiday*, which will forever be one of my favourites. It was the first time I wrote about dating and it was the most empowering, cathartic and beautiful experience. It made me realise I wanted to do more of it. Thank you to Camille Wyand for saying yes, for being the wonderful person that you are, for becoming such a good friend. Thank you to Thursday Dating and its founders, George Rawlings and Matthew McNeill Love, and HomeExchange and PR manager Jessica Poillucci for making the trip happen and giving me the idea.

Thank you to my family for always showing me that I am loved. I am so lucky to have you all by my side and think you are magic. Mum, you taught me to love reading and thus writing. You also inspire me daily to be my true self and showed me the power of being both smart and silly. Dad, I love how much you believe in me and that you always have such wise advice and funny jokes. You are both amazing role models for me. Kate, you make me laugh wildly and you always know what to say. I think you are the coolest and kindest person. Nana, you mean so much to me. As do my aunts, uncles, cousins and more on both sides of the pond.

Thank you too to my extended family who are now my family too, and I couldn't be happier about it: Matthew Bowman, Lana Gindina, Laura Bowman and Peter Bowman.

Thank you to my friends who bring me so much joy and love (and have listened to me talking about this book again and again. And of course talking about various romances and flings again and again. And again). Many of you also read early versions and your feedback meant the world to me. I am incredibly lucky to have such talented friends. Not to mention friends who will let me write about their love lives. Alex Bick, Alice Atherton, Alina Tolmatcheva, Amelia Hill-Smith, Andie Nishimi, Annie Bruce, Beth Newton, Chris, Dhara Patel, Eamonn Crowe, Ellie, Emilie Sampson, Emily Mills, Emma Beaumont, Eva Healy, George, Hannah, Hannah Ferrand, Hannah Gendler, Harriet Jones, Izzi Bailey, Jade Conroy, Jessica, Jessica Carpani, Juliet Cuell, Keshet Haslum, Laura Smyllie, Lauren, Leanne Atkinson, Nick, Rachel Cranshaw, Robbie Hodges, Sophie Littler, Shivani, Sloan Caldwell, Stacey Yuen, Tara Odeinde-Rothera and Zoë Cooper.

Thank you to my colleagues at the *Telegraph* who commissioned me, edited me, offered publishing advice and taught me so much. Including but not limited to: Ben Ross, Andrew Baker, Laura Powell, Alexis Giles, Victoria Young, Caroline Barrett-Haigh, Lucy Aspden, McKenna Grant, Keith Miller.

Thank you to my colleagues at *The Times*, especially the talented travel team. I feel extremely lucky to be part of it. Thank you for the commissions, edits and general mischief and merriment. Including but not limited to: Claire Irvin, Laura Jackson, Claudia Rowan, Lucy Perrin, Cathy Adams, Blossom Green, Huw Oliver, Liz Edwards, Gemma Bowes, Jenny Coad, Hannah Gravett, Min Sett Hein and Alexandra Whiting. And thanks too to new friends at *The Times* including Victoria Brzezinski, Roisin Kelly and Sean Russell.

Thank you to my housemates in London, Nice, Barcelona and at university.

Thank you to the many people I have met on my travels who have gone on to be dear friends, and even characters in this book. I hope our paths cross again in some corner of the world.

Thank you to the men that I have liked, loved and longed for. On the whole, I've been lucky.

Thank you to Taylor Swift. Who may have no idea who I am, but taught me the best thing to do with a break-up is to turn it into art.

Thank you to Frame and your incredible instructors who helped me get in the right mindset to write for hours (and even unknowingly helped me through one or two heartbreaks).

Thank you to the places where I wrote lots of this book, often with a cocktail or croissant in hand: Wild by Tart, Juliet's Quality Foods, Tooting Library, Backstory and Chestnut Bakery.

And thank you, reader, for being here on this journey with me. Thank you for choosing to read this book. I will continue to pinch myself over that fact for the rest of my life.